God, Satan, and Angels

God, Satan, and Angels

by
John MacArthur, Jr.

WORD OF GRACE COMMUNICATIONS
P.O. Box 4000
Panorama City, CA 91412

All Scripture quotations, unless noted otherwise, are from the *New Scofield Reference Bible*, King James Version. Copyright © 1967 by Oxford University Press, Inc. Reprinted by permission.

ISBN: 0-8024-5385-6

1 2 3 4 5 6 Printing/LC/Year 93 92 91 90 89

Printed in the United States of America

Contents

These Bible studies are taken from messages delivered by Pastor-Teacher John MacArthur, Jr., at Grace Community Church in Panorama City, California. These messages have been combined into a 9-tape album titled *God, Satan, and Angels*. You may purchase this series either in an attractive vinyl cassette album or as individual cassettes. To purchase these tapes, request the album *God, Satan, and Angels*, or ask for the tapes by their individual GC numbers. Please consult the current price list; then, send your order, making your check payable to:

WORD OF GRACE COMMUNICATIONS
P.O. Box 4000
Panorama City, CA 91412

Or call the following toll-free number:
1-800-55-GRACE

1
God—Part 1

Outline

Introduction
A. God Is the Eternal Creator
B. God Is a Merciful Refuge
C. God Is a Just Judge

Lesson
I. God—Is He?
   A. The Debate on God's Existence
      1. The invention of God
         a) Fear of nature
         b) Fear of relationships
         c) Fear of death
      2. The elimination of God
   B. The Defense of God's Existence
      1. The arguments
         a) Teleological
         b) Ontological
         c) Aesthetical
         d) Volitional
         e) Moral
         f) Cosmological
            (1) Examining the equations
            (2) Examining the effects
               (*a*) The cause of limitless space must be infinite
               (*b*) The cause of endless time must be eternal
               (*c*) The cause of perpetual motion must be powerful
               (*d*) The cause of complexity must be omniscient
               (*e*) The cause of consciousness must be personal
               (*f*) The cause of feeling must be emotional

(*g*) The cause of will must be volitional
(*h*) The cause of ethical values must be moral
(*i*) The cause of religious values must be spiritual
(*j*) The cause of beauty must be aesthetic
(*k*) The cause of righteousness must be holy
(*l*) The cause of justice must be just
(*m*) The cause of love must be loving
(*n*) The cause of life must be living
   2. The assurance
II. God—Who Is He?
  A. His Person Defended
  B. His Person Defined
    1. God is spirit
     a) Numbers 23:19
     b) John 4:24
     c) Luke 24:39
    2. God is one
     a) Defended by Jesus
     b) Defended by Paul
       (1) The Corinthians' problem
       (2) Paul's solution
    3. God is three
     a) Implicit evidence in the Old Testament
       (1) Genesis 1:1
       (2) Numbers 6:24-26
     b) Explicit evidence in the New Testament
       (1) Matthew 3:16-17
       (2) John 14:16-17
       (3) 1 Corinthians 12:4-6
       (4) 2 Corinthians 13:14
       (5) 1 Peter 1:2
III. God—What Is He Like?
  A. He Is Unchanging (Immutable)
    1. The concept
     a) Psalm 102:26
     b) Malachi 3:6
     c) James 1:17
    2. The contrast
     a) The heavens change
     b) The earth changes
     c) The ungodly change
     d) The saints change
     e) The demons change

3. The comfort
   a) 2 Peter 3:9
   b) Romans 11:29
   c) 2 Timothy 2:13
   d) Jeremiah 31:3
   e) Isaiah 54:10
   f) Isaiah 46:10
4. The confusion
   a) Didn't God change His mind about Nineveh?
   b) Didn't God change His mind about creating man?

Conclusion

Introduction

A. God Is the Eternal Creator

Psalm 90:2 says, "Before the mountains were brought forth, or ever thou hadst formed the earth and the world, even from everlasting to everlasting, thou art God." That verse contains great doctrinal truth. "Thou art God" tells us that God is the only God. "From everlasting to everlasting" tells us that God is eternal. And the phrase "before the mountains were brought forth, or ever thou hadst formed the earth and the world" tells us that God is the Creator.

B. God Is a Merciful Refuge

Moses, the author of Psalm 90, contrasted the eternal character of God to the frailty of man. Verse 10 says, "The days of our years are three-score years and ten [seventy years]; and if, by reason of strength, they be fourscore [eighty] years, yet is their strength labor and sorrow; for it is soon cut off, and we fly away."

In verse 1 Moses says, "Lord, thou hast been our dwelling place in all generations." When faced with their own inadequacies and frailties, the people of Israel realized they had strength only when they sought refuge in God's strength.

Although they were God's people, the nation needed God's mercy. So Moses prayed, "Satisfy us early with thy mercy" (v. 14).

C. God Is a Just Judge

God is not only the merciful benefactor of the godly, but also the judge of the ungodly. Psalm 90:7 refers to the terrible power of God's anger and wrath.

Psalm 90 pictures God as the eternal Creator who blesses the righteous and punishes the unrighteous. We who accept God and His revelation agree with that portrait, but many contend that Christians have invented that God. Some go to the extreme of claiming that everyone who is religious has merely postulated their religion or been victimized by some forefather who did. In their opinion there is no supernatural realm.

Lesson

I. GOD—IS HE?

A. The Debate on God's Existence

1. The invention of God

Sigmund Freud, the progenitor of modern psychoanalysis, believed that man created God, not the other way around. In his book *The Future of an Illusion* (N.Y.: W. W. Norton, 1961), Freud said that man desperately needs security because we have deep-seated fears of living in a threatening world in which we have little control over our circumstances. He believed that we invent God as a protective father, and he suggested three reasons for our doing so.

a) Fear of nature

Man fears the unpredictability, impersonality, and ruthlessness of nature. Because we all see the frightful reality of disease, famine, and disasters against which we have only a nominal defense, Freud assumed that we postulate a supernatural being who can deliver us.

An illustration of that is a native who lives on a volcanic island. Suddenly he hears rumblings and the ground begins to shake. He walks outside his hut and sees lava blowing out the top of the volcano. He realizes that shoring up his hut and comforting his wife and children won't help. Since there seems to be no way out, he looks for a supernatural being to save him from the terror of nature.

b) Fear of relationships

Because we often feel used by other people, Freud assumed that we conjure up a divine umpire—a cosmic God with a super whistle who ultimately stops play and penalizes people for what they have done. We all want someone who can right the wrongs of injustice.

c) Fear of death

Freud claimed that we want a heavenly Father who will take us to a happy place, which we call heaven. We don't want to face the fact that life will end one day.

Freud's view of God is that there is no God, except as a figment of our imagination. There is no proof for his hypothesis, yet myriads have believed it.

2. The elimination of God

Freud's view of religion is rather simplistic. A careful examination of human religions reveals that the gods man creates are rarely of the delivering kind, but usually have an oppressive nature that needs continual appeasement. I disagree with Freud; I don't believe that man has invented God. If man had his way he would rather that God did not exist.

The first thing Adam and Eve did after they sinned was to hide from God (Gen. 3:8). To be free from a God who calls sinners into accountability has been a constant goal for mankind throughout history. Romans 1 tells us that all men and women know that God exists "because that which may be known of God is manifest in them" (v. 19). "They knew God" (v. 21), but "they did not like to retain God in their knowledge" (v. 28). Man has not made God; man wishes that God did not exist.

The gods spawned by false religions are not protecting gods; they are fearsome gods. Women in India who drown their babies in the Ganges River don't think of their god as a savior—they see it as a fearful ogre they must appease. If man invents gods, he surely invents the wrong kinds! Such gods are actually a representation of demonic activity.

B. The Defense of God's Existence

Evidence for God's existence is abundant. To postulate that there is no God and to invent a theory attempting to prove that God was created by man ignores valid theological arguments for the existence of God. Theologians propose many reasons for believing in the existence of God.

1. The arguments

   a) Teleological

   The Greek word *teleios* means "perfection," "result," or "end." When we look at something that has been finished or perfected, we conclude its resulting design must have had a designer. You can't take your watch apart, put all the pieces in a bag, shake it, and then hear the watch tick. A piano didn't just happen to come together because an elephant ran into a tree while a harpist was playing his harp on one of the limbs! Design implies a designer.

   b) Ontological

   Ontōs is a Greek participle from the verb translated "to be." This argument reasons that man's ability to conceive of an absolutely perfect Being implies the reality and existence of that Being.

c) Aesthetical

Because there is beauty and truth in the world, it is logical to assume that somewhere in the universe is a standard upon which beauty and truth are based.

d) Volitional

Because man faces a myriad of choices and exercises volition, it is logical to assume that there must be an infinite will somewhere. The world exists as an expression of that will.

e) Moral

That we know there is right and wrong suggests the necessity of an absolute standard.

f) Cosmological

(1) Examining the equations

Cosmology is the argument of cause and effect. The world and universe exist, and we conclude that someone made it. That makes more sense than believing that everything came out of nothing—that at one point nothing equaled all things —which is essentially what the theory of evolution says. As we carefully examine the world, we learn more about the One who made it.

(2) Examining the effects

(*a*) The cause of limitless space must be infinite.

(*b*) The cause of endless time must be eternal.

(*c*) The cause of perpetual motion must be powerful.

(*d*) The cause of complexity must be omniscient.

(*e*) The cause of consciousness must be personal.

(*f*) The cause of feeling must be emotional.

(*g*) The cause of will must be volitional.

(*h*) The cause of ethical values must be moral.

(*i*) The cause of religious values must be spiritual.

(*j*) The cause of beauty must be aesthetic.

(*k*) The cause of righteousness must be holy.

(*l*) The cause of justice must be just.

(*m*) The cause of love must be loving.

(*n*) The cause of life must be living.

Our world gives evidence that there must be a God who is the cause of all those qualities, which are merely reflections of His character. And the Bible substantiates every one.

Based on all those arguments you would think that refusing to believe that God exists is a sign of ignorance. Psalm 14:1 supports that reasoning: "The fool hath said in his heart, There is no God" (cf. Ps. 53:1).

The Despair of Life Without God

I am convinced of the existence of God not only because we have no other way to explain anything in the world, but also because we need Him so badly. Contrary to Freud, the fact that we need God may be evidence for Him, not evidence against Him. That need is illustrated by the story of an atheist who, in the midst of a difficult situation, began to call to God. Someone who knew he was an atheist heard him and said, "Why are you calling on God?" The atheist replied, "If there isn't a God, there ought to be for times like this!"

People who deny the existence or relevance of God often lead lives of great despair. If you study the well-known philosophical atheists and deists of the world, you will see that many developed a bleak outlook on life here and after death.

1. Voltaire—An aristocratic woman who was old and blind wrote to Voltaire in the hopes that he could dispel her pessimistic view of life and offer some comfort. He replied, "I think we [human beings] are indeed contemptible creatures. . . . I exhort you to enjoy as much as you can life, which isn't much" (Norman L. Torrey, *The Spirit of Voltaire* [N.Y.: Columbia University, 1938], p. 216).

2. H. G. Wells—"I do not believe I have any personal immortality. . . . I feel I have to do something . . . and then I am finished, and finished altogether. Then my substance returns to the common lot" (*The Undying Fire and Philosophical and Theological Speculations*, "First and Last Things" [N.Y.: Charles Scribner's Sons, 1925], p. 261).

3. Mark Twain—Samuel L. Clemens became notoriously cynical in the later years of his life. His *What Is Man? And Other Philosophical Writings* (L.A.: University of California, 1973) contains some of the most disparaging statements against mankind ever written. At the heading of the third chapter of *The Tragedy of Pudd'nhead Wilson* (1894) he wrote, "Whoever has lived long enough to find out what life is, knows how deep a debt of gratitude we owe to Adam, the first benefactor of our race. He brought death into the world." He also wrote, "Man was made at the end of the week's work when God was tired" (Albert Bigelow Paine, *Mark Twain: A Biography*, vol. 3 [N.Y.: Harper & Brothers, 1912], p. 1195).

4. Bertrand Russell—"That Man is the product of causes which had no prevision of the end they were achieving; that his origin, his growth, his hopes and fears, his loves and his beliefs, are but the outcome of accidental collocations of atoms; that no fire, no heroism, no intensity of thought and feeling, can preserve an individual life beyond the grave; that all the labours of the ages, all the devotion, all the inspiration, all the noonday brightness of human genius, are destined to extinction in the

vast death of the solar system, and that the whole temple of man's achievement must inevitably be buried beneath the debris of a universe in ruins—all these things, if not quite beyond dispute, are yet so nearly certain, that no philosophy which rejects them can hope to stand" ("A Free Man's Worship" in *Selected Papers of Bertrand Russell* [N.Y.: The Modern Library, 1927], p. 3).

The evidence shows that God exists. How sad it is for people to forsake the evidence and arrive at such a bleak outlook.

2. The assurance

In marked contrast, the results of faith in God are bright. The psalmist said, "Yea, though I walk through the valley of the shadow of death, I will fear no evil; for thou art with me" (Ps. 23:4). He also said, "Thou wilt show me the path of life. In thy presence is fullness of joy; at thy right hand there are pleasures for evermore" (Ps. 16:11).

II. GOD—WHO IS HE?

A. His Person Defended

Albert Einstein admitted to the existence of a cosmic force in the universe but concluded that it is unknowable (*Cosmic Religion* [N.Y.: Covici, Friede, 1931], pp. 47-48). He was mistaken.

The Bible reveals that God is a Person. It uses personal titles to describe Him: He is called a father, a shepherd, a friend, and a counselor. The Bible also uses personal pronouns to refer to God. The Hebrew and Greek texts refer to God as "He"—never as "it." And the Bible shows God to be a person because He thinks, acts, feels, and speaks—He communicates. All the evidence of Scripture indicates He is a person, and all the evidence of creation and our personhood indicates we came from Him.

B. His Person Defined

    1. God is spirit

        a) Numbers 23:19—God's spiritual nature is implied by the statement: "God is not a man."

        b) John 4:24—"God is a spirit, and those who worship Him must worship in spirit and truth" (NASB*).

        c) Luke 24:39—Jesus said, "A spirit hath not flesh and bones." God doesn't have a body.

Accommodating the Message to the Man

Even though God doesn't have a body, the Bible says such things as, "The eyes of the Lord . . . run to and fro through the whole earth" (Zech. 4:10), "Is my hand shortened at all, that it cannot redeem?" (Isa. 50:2), and "Thou hast a mighty arm" (Ps. 89:13). We call those descriptions *anthropomorphisms*. That word comes from two Greek words: *anthrōpos* (man) and *morphē* (form). References to a human form attributed to God are an accommodation God has made to our finite understanding.

Let me caution you to avoid using anthropomorphisms to reduce God to a man, as some of the cults have done. Psalm 91:4 says God covers us with His feathers, but that doesn't mean He's a bird. God is not a man or a bird—He is spirit.

First Timothy 1:17 refers to God as invisible. No man has ever seen God (John 1:18). In Exodus 33:20 God says, "No man [can] see me, and live." In the Old Testament God represented Himself by the *Shekinah*—the divine light, fire, and cloud. In the New Testament He represented Himself in the form of Jesus Christ (John 1:14, 18). Jesus said, "He that hath seen me hath seen the Father" (John 14:9). God may choose to manifest

---

* *New American Standard Bible*

Himself in some way by limiting Himself to something visible, but that is not the totality of His Person.

2. God is one

There is only one God. Moses made that clear in the following statement, the key to Israel's religious convictions: "Hear, O Israel: The Lord our God is one Lord" (Deut. 6:4). The people of Israel lived in the midst of polytheistic societies, yet they were to believe in only one God.

a) Defended by Jesus

Jesus claimed to be God—does that mean He claimed to be another God? No. He reiterated what Moses said about the oneness of God: "The first of all the commandments is: Hear, O Israel: The Lord our God is one Lord; and thou shalt love the Lord thy God with all thy heart, and with all thy soul, and with all thy mind, and with all thy strength" (Mark 12:29-30). If Jesus were claiming that He was another God, He would never have made that statement. He would have had to say, "Split your allegiance between the two of us."

When Jesus said we are to love God with undivided commitment, He was agreeing with the Old Testament statement that there is only one God. But at the same time (though not explicitly in this particular passage), He was claiming to be that very God.

b) Defended by Paul

In 1 Corinthians 8 Paul had to solve a problem the Corinthian Christians faced because they lived in a pagan society that worshiped many false gods.

(1) The Corinthians' problem

The pagans would offer food to their false gods as an act of worship. It was a common practice for the priests to take the food that wasn't actually consumed on the altar and sell it in a market they

18

ran outside the temple. Christians who had been saved out of idolatry were offended when they discovered that other Christians were eating food that had been offered to idols. They especially were offended when fellow believers offered them some at a meal.

(2) Paul's solution

To correct the problem Paul said, "As concerning, therefore, the eating of those things that are offered in sacrifice unto idols, we know that an idol is nothing in the world" (1 Cor. 8:4). Paul's argument was that since an idol represented a nonexistent god, there was nothing wrong with eating the food. Then he said, "There is no other God but one. For though there be that are called gods, whether in heaven or in earth (as there are gods many, and lords many), but to us there is but one God, the Father, of whom are all things, and we in him; and one Lord Jesus Christ, by whom are all things, and we by him" (vv. 4-6). How can all things be by God the Father, in whom we are, and by the Lord Jesus Christ, by whom we are? Because they are one and the same. God is one (1 Tim. 2:5).

The "gods" in Psalm 82

In Psalm 82:6 God says to the rulers of Israel, "Ye are gods." Does that mean there are many gods? No. In speaking to the judges of Israel, God was not referring to their essence but their office. The judges represented God as they judged Israel. They were to judge the people as if God were judging them. Nevertheless the psalmist made it clear that they were not equal to God for he immediately said, "But ye shall die like men" (v. 7). To the Holy God alone he appeals, saying, "Arise, O God, judge the earth" (v. 8).

3. God is three

God is one, yet exists as three distinct persons. That is revealed in the Bible from beginning to end.

a) Implicit evidence in the Old Testament

   (1) Genesis 1:1—"In the beginning God." The Hebrew word translated "God" is *Elohim*. An *im* ending on a Hebrew word means it's plural. Genesis 1 presents a singular God who is expressed as a plurality.

   (2) Numbers 6:24-26—"The Lord bless thee, and keep thee; the Lord make his face shine upon thee, and be gracious unto thee; the Lord lift up his countenance upon thee, and give thee peace." The three references to the Lord could be an allusion to the Trinity.

   Other implicit evidence can be found by studying how the word "Lord" is used in Genesis 19:24 and Psalm 110.

b) Explicit evidence in the New Testament

   (1) Matthew 3:16-17—As Jesus was being baptized by John the Baptist, the Holy Spirit descended on Him like a dove. The Father replied, "This is my beloved Son, in whom I am well pleased" (v. 17). We see the Father, Son, and Holy Spirit together in the same scene.

   (2) John 14:16-17—Jesus said, "I will pray the Father, and he shall give you another Comforter, that he may abide with you forever; even the Spirit of truth."

   (3) 1 Corinthians 12:4-6—"There are diversities of gifts, but the same Spirit. And there are differences of administrations, but the same Lord. And there are diversities of operations, but it is the same God who worketh all in all."

   (4) 2 Corinthians 13:14—"The grace of the Lord Jesus Christ, and the love of God, and the communion of the Holy Spirit be with you all. Amen."

(5) 1 Peter 1:2—Peter said believers are "elect according to the foreknowledge of God, the Father, through sanctification of the Spirit, unto obedience and sprinkling of the blood of Jesus Christ."

God is one, yet He is three. That is a mystery, yet it is not unparalleled in our experience. An egg is one, yet it consists of three parts: a shell, a white, and a yolk. Water is one, yet it exists in three states: solid, liquid, and gas. Nevertheless those are imperfect illustrations because God is greater than we can fully comprehend.

III. GOD—WHAT IS HE LIKE?

A. He Is Unchanging (Immutable)

1. The concept

   a) Psalm 102:26—In explaining the difference between the heavens and God, the psalmist said, "They shall perish, but thou shalt endure. . . . Thou art the same, and thy years shall have no end."

   b) Malachi 3:6—God said, "I am the Lord, I change not."

   c) James 1:17—"Every good gift and every perfect gift is from above, and cometh down from the Father of lights, with whom is no variableness, neither shadow of turning."

2. The contrast

   Change is either for the better or for the worse. Yet both are inconceivable in God because He doesn't change. That sets Him apart from everything else because everything changes.

   a) The heavens change

   The heavens move about, following their courses. Scientists tell us there are exploding stars—new worlds are being created all the time. Revelation 6-19

21

gives us a drastic picture of the extreme changes the heavens will undergo until they are eventually dissolved by fire (Rev. 8:12; 2 Pet. 3:7, 10, 12). The stars will fall, the sun will go out, the moon will turn a bloody hue, and the heavens will roll up like a scroll (Rev. 6:12-17).

b) The earth changes

Man has been changing the face of the earth with his bulldozers and the atmosphere with pollution. Revelation 6-19 details the changes the earth will undergo: the seas will be polluted, plant life will die, and people will die. Earthquakes and hailstorms will drastically change the face of the earth (Rev. 6:1-11; 8:3-11; 9:13-19). The earth was changed once by a flood; it will be changed again as it is consumed with fervent heat (2 Pet. 3:6-7).

c) The ungodly change

What unbelievers now believe is a happy or acceptable way to live they will find to be a tragic existence when they realize they will spend an eternity without God.

d) The saints change

There are times when our love for Christ burns and we obey Him, but there are other times when it smolders and we disobey Him. David said, "The God of my rock; in him will I trust" (2 Sam. 22:3). But he also said, "I shall now perish . . . by the hand of Saul" (1 Sam. 27:1).

e) The demons change

Jude 6 says that the demons "kept not their first [angelic] estate."

Everything in the universe changes except God and Christ, which reveals His equality with God. Hebrews 13:8 says, "Jesus Christ [is] the same yesterday, and today, and forever."

22

3. The comfort

What does the unchanging character of God mean to us as Christians? Comfort. Since God loves us now, He loves us forever. Since He forgave us, He forgave us forever. Since He saved us, He saved us forever.

a) 2 Peter 3:9—"The Lord is not slack concerning his promise."

b) Romans 11:29—"The gifts and calling of God are without repentance." That means God doesn't change His mind.

c) 2 Timothy 2:13—"If we believe not, yet he abides faithful; he cannot deny himself."

d) Jeremiah 31:3—God said of Israel, "I have loved thee with an everlasting love."

e) Isaiah 54:10—God also said of Israel, "The mountains shall depart, and the hills be removed, but my kindness shall not depart from thee, neither shall the covenant of my peace be removed."

f) Isaiah 46:10—God said, "My counsel shall stand."

For us to be rightly related to an unchanging God we have to undergo a drastic change. Jesus said to Nicodemus, "Except a man be born again, he cannot see the kingdom of God" (John 3:3).

4. The confusion

Several scriptures such as Genesis 6:6, Amos 7:6, and Jonah 3:10 say that God repented. Yet Numbers 23:19 says, "God is not a man, that he lie; neither the son of man, that he should repent." How do we reconcile those scriptures? We know that God Himself doesn't change (Mal. 3:6). However, He may will something to change under certain circumstances.

a) Didn't God change His mind about Nineveh?

God commissioned Jonah to warn Nineveh of impending judgment because of its wickedness (Jonah 1:2-3). Jonah rebelled, but God got him there through a miraculous ride inside a large fish (1:17–2:10). When he arrived, Jonah preached and the people repented (3:1-5). Verse 10 says, "God saw their works, that they turned from their evil way; and God repented of the evil that he said that he would do unto them, and he did it not." But God didn't change; Nineveh did.

b) Didn't God change His mind about creating man?

When God looked on the pre-Flood civilization, "it repented the Lord that he had made man on earth, and it grieved him at his heart. And the Lord said, I will destroy man whom I have created from the face of the earth" (Gen. 6:6-7). God made man to do good, but man did evil. Yet God Himself hasn't changed; He continues to reward good and punish evil.

You can't blame the sun for melting wax and hardening clay. The problem is in the substance of those objects, not in the sun. The way a man stands before God dictates what happens to him. Have you ever ridden a bike against the wind? It's a struggle until you turn around and coast with the force of the wind. You can't say that the wind changed; you changed in relation to the wind. God never changes. He will continue to reward good and punish evil. How you view His actions depends on where you are in His grace and will.

Conclusion

The Bible says to the believer, "My God shall supply all your need" (Phil. 4:19). But to the unbeliever God says, "The soul that sinneth, it shall die" (Ezek. 18:20). Romans 6:23 says, "The wages of sin is death." Psalm 119:89 says, "Forever, O Lord, thy word is settled in heaven." God never changes. To some that truth brings great joy. For others it ought to cause fear and a desire to repent from evil.

Focusing on the Facts

1. What was Freud's view of God in relation to man (see p. 10)?
2. What is the nature of the gods man invents (see p. 11)?
3. What is man's natural response to the true God (Rom. 1:28; see p. 11)?
4. Cite the theological arguments for the existence of God, and give a brief explanation of each (see pp. 12-14).
5. Whom does the Bible identify as a fool (Ps. 14:1; see p. 14)?
6. What is God, according to the evidence of Scripture (see p. 16)?
7. Why does Scripture attribute physical characteristics to God (see p. 17)?
8. What was unique about Israel's worship compared to the societies around them (see p. 18)?
9. What did Jesus support when He quoted Deuteronomy 6:4-5 in Mark 12:29-30 (see p. 18)?
10. What is significant about 1 Corinthians 8:4-6 (see p. 19)?
11. Why were the rulers of Israel called "gods" in Psalm 82:6 (see p. 19)?
12. Cite Old and New Testament scriptures that give evidence for the existence of the Trinity (see pp. 20-21).
13. What aspects of creation make immutability an attribute unique to God (see pp. 21-22)?
14. What does God's unchanging character mean to the godly (see p. 23)?
15. Explain the circumstances when the Bible says God repented. Do those instances mean He changed (see pp. 23-24)?

Pondering the Principles

1. The world is full of either philosophic or pragmatic atheists— the former don't believe in God; the latter live as if His existence had no effect on them. In sharing Christ with an atheist, it's helpful to know which kind of atheist he is. Determine how you might alter your presentation of God's truth to match the type of person with whom you're speaking. For some ideas, compare Stephen's address to the Jewish religious leaders (Acts 7) and Paul's address to Gentile philosophers (Acts 17:18-34).

2. Jesus' identification with God presupposes His equality with Him. Look up the following verses that discuss the nature of their equality and fill in the blanks.

   a) To _____ Him was to _____ the Father (John 8:19; 14:7).

   b) To _____ Him was to _____ the Father (John 15:23).

   c) To _____ Him was to _____ the Father (John 12:44; 14:1).

   d) To _____ Him was to _____ the Father (John 12:45; 14:9).

   e) To _____ Him was to _____ the Father (John 5:23; 17:5).

   f) To _____ Him was to _____ the Father (Matt. 10:40; Mark 9:37).

   g) To _____ Him was to _____ the Father (John 8:42; 14:23).

3. We change because we are human. But for the Christian, change need not carry a negative connotation. What kind of change is occurring in us for God's glory (Rom. 8:29; 12:2; 2 Cor. 3:18; Col. 1:27)? What areas of your life need to change for the pleasure of the Lord?

2
God—Part 2

Outline

Introduction
A. The Importance of Knowing God
B. The Importance of Making God Known
   1. To those who deny the knowledge of God
   2. To those who distort the knowledge of God

Review
  I. God—Is He?
 II. God—Who Is He?
III. God—What Is He Like?
    A. God Is Unchanging (Immutable)

Lesson
    B. God Is Everywhere (Omnipresent)
       1. Attempts to confine God
          a) To the Temple in Jerusalem
          b) To the mountains
          c) To the heavens
       2. Answers to major objections
          a) Wouldn't the sin in the world defile an omnipresent God?
          b) Doesn't the Bible say God is near to some and far from others?
             (1) His relational presence
             (2) His symbolic presence
       3. Applications for all people
          a) Believers
             (1) Comfort
             (2) Support

        (3) A shield against temptation
        (4) A motivation to holiness
           (*a*) Preventing impurity
           (*b*) Promoting integrity
              i) David
              ii) Job
  b) Unbelievers
      (1) Psalm 21:8
      (2) Amos 9:2-4
      (3) Obadiah 4
      (4) Job 34:21-22
      (5) Proverbs 15:11
      (6) Hebrews 4:13
      (7) Isaiah 65:12
      (8) Proverbs 15:3

C. God Is All Powerful (Omnipotent)
  1. The extent of God's power
    a) God can do anything
    b) God can do anything effortlessly
    c) God can do anything He wants
  2. The expression of God's power
    a) Creation
    b) Preservation
    c) Redemption
    d) Resurrection
  3. The experience of God's power
    a) By the believer
      (1) The basis of our worship
      (2) The basis of daily confidence
      (3) The basis of resurrection hope
      (4) The basis of comfort
      (5) The basis of victory
      (6) The basis of assurance
         (*a*) John 10:28-29
         (*b*) Romans 8:33, 35, 38-39
         (*c*) 2 Timothy 1:12
      (7) The basis of humility
    b) By the unbeliever
      (1) 1 Corinthians 10:22
      (2) Job 9:4
      (3) 2 Thessalonians 1:7-9
      (4) Hebrews 10:31

Conclusion

Introduction

A. The Importance of Knowing God

A helpful book on the nature of God is *The Knowledge of the Holy* by A. W. Tozer (San Francisco: Harper & Row, 1961). In it Tozer says, "The history of mankind will probably show that no people has ever risen above its religion, and man's spiritual history will positively demonstrate that no religion has ever been greater than its idea of God. Worship is pure or base as the worshiper entertains high or low thoughts of God. For this reason the gravest question before the Church is always God Himself, and the most portentous fact about any man is not what he at a given time may say or do, but what he in his deep heart conceives God to be like" (p. 9). What mankind needs most is a proper understanding of God.

B. The Importance of Making God Known

Consequently, the most important message the church can present is the truth about God.

1. To those who deny the knowledge of God

   Some people do not believe in God; they are considered philosophical atheists. Others believe in Him but don't act like they do; they are in a sense practical atheists. They all need to know that they can know God personally.

2. To those who distort the knowledge of God

   Many people, including some Christians, have misconceptions about God. That's a serious matter because believing the wrong thing about God is essentially idolatry. The common understanding of idolatry is that it is bowing down to a small figure or worshiping in some ornate pagan temple. But idolatry is much broader: it is thinking anything about God that isn't true.

In its fullest sense idolatry is the creation of a god. But in a secondary sense it is transforming God into something that He isn't. In Psalm 50:21 God says, "Thou thoughtest that I was altogether such an one as thyself." Man has made God in his own likeness. So the essence of idolatry is entertaining thoughts about God that are unworthy of Him.

Review

I. GOD—IS HE? (see pp. 10-16)

II. GOD—WHO IS HE? (see pp. 16-21)

III. GOD—WHAT IS HE LIKE?

The only way we can know what God is like is to discover what He has revealed about Himself in the Bible. The revelation of God's nature falls into different categories of attributes, which are definitions of His character.

Attempting to Comprehend the Incomprehensible

God is incomprehensible. He is infinite—there is no end to Him. So instead of asking, *what is God?* we start with the question, *what is God like?* We can't begin to know exactly what God is. But we can find out what He is like through what He has revealed to us and what we've observed.

However we're to beware of the danger of judging God by human standards. For example, when God's love doesn't behave like human love, we could conclude that He isn't loving. But that's making human love the absolute standard and trying to make God's love measure up to that.

To define God in terms we can understand, we often have to state what He is not. For example, when we say that God is holy, we mean He has no sin. We have to see Him that way because we can't conceive of absolute holiness, whereas we're all too familiar with sin. We can't begin to understand the limitless nature of God without knowing that He doesn't have any limits.

30

God is infinite, and as such He probably has an infinite number of attributes. We will concentrate our study on just a few of them.

A. God Is Unchanging (Immutable) (see pp. 21-24)

Lesson

B. God Is Everywhere (Omnipresent)

God is infinite. There is no end to Him. His being fills up endless infinity. In Jeremiah 23:24 God says, "Do not I fill heaven and earth?" In 1 Kings 8:27 Solomon says, "Will God indeed dwell on the earth? Behold, the heaven and heaven of heavens cannot contain thee; how much less this house that I have built!" God is before all things and after all things, within all things and without all things. He has no limits. Just as His wisdom and knowledge are unsearchable (Rom. 11:33), so is His presence.

1. Attempts to confine God

Throughout history people have tried to confine God.

a) To the Temple in Jerusalem

Although Solomon correctly said that God could not dwell in the heaven and earth—let alone in the Temple—many of the people believed He dwelt in the actual structure of the Temple. However, it was simply the seat of His majesty on earth—the symbol of His presence, not the sole location of it.

b) To the mountains

The Syrians worshiped the god of the valleys and assumed the God of Israel was the god of the mountains (1 Kings 20:23). They supposed Israel confined their religious activities to the mountains so they might be nearer to their God. Clearly mountains such as Mount Sinai, Mount Gerizim, and Jerusalem, which is situated on a plateau, played an important

31

role in the worship of Israel. The prophets went up into the mountains to pray, as did Jesus. So a simple conclusion would have been that Israel worshiped only the God of the mountains.

c) To the heavens

Many professing Christians see God as being confined to heaven. They imagine Him sitting on a brilliant throne off in some celestial palace, but not anywhere else.

2. Answers to major objections

a) Wouldn't the sin in the world defile an omnipresent God?

Some argue that if God is everywhere, He must be impure because He would be defiled by the impure things that touch Him. Without a doubt God is in all places and in everything. As a holy God He enters the hearts of sinners to inspect them and convict them of sin. He also is in hell to execute judgment, for Matthew 10:28 says He "is able to destroy both soul and body in hell."

While God's essence is everywhere, He never mingles with any impurity. He is like the sun's rays. A sunbeam may fall on a manure pile in a field, but the manure pile can't defile the sunbeam. In the same sense nothing can defile God—He is not mixed with anything. Jesus came into the world and lived among sinners. Yet the apostle John said of Him: "In him is no sin" (1 John 3:5). He was among sinful men and women yet totally undefiled by them.

b) Doesn't the Bible say God is near to some and far from others?

Isaiah 55:6 exhorts people to call on the Lord "while he is near." Elsewhere the Old Testament says that Israel's rebellion caused God to be far from them (Prov. 15:29; Isa. 29:13). How can God be both near to and far from people when He is everywhere all the time?

(1) His relational presence

It is important that we see the distinction between God's essence and His relation to people. He is everywhere in His essence, but only in certain places relationally. Specifically, He dwells in the hearts of the godly. When we become Christians, Christ takes up residence in us. He fills us with His fullness (Eph. 3:19). Likewise the Spirit fills us with His fullness (Eph. 5:18). Colossians 1:27 says, "Christ in you [is your] hope of glory." But before He ever indwelt us relationally, His essence convicted us of sin and saved us.

Genesis 11:5 says, "The Lord came down [from heaven] to see the city and the tower." That doesn't mean that God left one place and came to another; but from the people's perspective, God gave the city His immediate attention.

(2) His symbolic presence

The Old Testament tells us that God dwelt between the wings of the cherubim above the Ark of the Covenant in either the Tabernacle or the Temple. Those were locations where God symbolically established the throne of His majesty. Today the throne of God is represented by the church, which is made up of believers. In the millennial kingdom the presence of God will be represented by Christ ruling on the throne of David in Jerusalem. In heaven He will be represented by the throne in Revelation 4-5. But the symbol of God's presence is never the prison of His essence.

33

3. Applications for all people

   a) Believers

   As Christians, how do we benefit from knowing that
   God is always present in our lives both essentially
   and relationally?

   (1) Comfort

   It's comforting to know that God is always present. No matter what trial you may have to endure, He is there. There are times when He
   doesn't seem to be near, but He's no further away
   then than He's ever been. God's promise to you
   is, "I will never leave thee, nor forsake thee"
   (Heb. 13:5). We know He means that because as
   we've learned, He can't lie.

   Philippians 4:5-6 says, "The Lord is at hand. Be
   anxious for nothing." I believe that that is not referring to Christ's second coming, but to His
   present comforting ministry to us. He is present
   all the time.

   A Christian can't ever be separated from God
   (Rom. 8:35-39). No one can be separated from the
   presence of God, and a believer can't be separated from a relationship with God. Enoch is an example of that unbroken fellowship. He walked
   with God on earth and one day God took him up
   to heaven (Gen. 5:24).

   (2) Support

   When God called Moses to proclaim His message
   and lead Israel out of bondage, Moses protested
   because of his lack of speaking abilities (Ex. 4:10).
   But God said, "I will be with thy mouth" (v. 12).
   That's a practical aspect of God's presence. He is
   present in support of our service.

   Jesus said to His disciples, "Go ye, therefore, and
   teach all nations, baptizing them in the name of

the Father, and of the Son, and of the Holy Spirit, teaching them to observe all things whatsoever I have commanded you; and, lo, I am with you always" (Matt. 28:19-20). He is always there to support us in service to Him.

People often doubt they have the power to witness for Christ. Instead they want the pastor to do their witnessing for them. But the people have the same resource as the pastor. The power of God is present for all His people.

(3) A shield against temptation

Whenever Satan wants to tempt a Christian, he has to clear it with God (Job. 1:6-12; Luke 22:31). First Corinthians 10:13 says, "There hath no temptation taken you but such as is common to man; but God is faithful, who will not permit you to be tempted above that ye are able, but will, with the temptation, also make the way to escape, that ye may be able to bear it." Nothing will ever come a believer's way without his having the God-given strength to resist. Each believer is at a different level of maturity, and different temptations will have different results. You may be able to handle something that might cause another person to crumble. But God meets every individual at his own level to defend and strengthen him against temptations.

(4) A motivation to holiness

(a) Preventing impurity

To know God is always present is to know that everything we do, we do in His presence. When we sin—whether a sin of thought, word, or action—we sin in the presence of God. For the most part, people prefer to sin when someone isn't watching. We may not be so careful around our family or friends because they're already aware of our problems. But aside from them we become quickly embarrassed when caught. But realize this: whenever you sin, it's as if you've ascended to the throne room of God, walked up to the foot of His throne, and sinned right there. Whatever you do, you do in the presence of God. That's a sobering thought!

(b) Promoting integrity

    i) David

        David said of God, "Thou compassest my path and my lying down, and art acquainted with all my ways" (Ps. 139:3). That knowledge helped to keep David pure. When you are tempted to sin, remember that God is with you.

    ii) Job

        Job said, "Doth not he see my ways?" (Job. 31:4). That was the basis of Job's integrity.

        Proverbs 3:6 says, "In all thy ways acknowledge him." In everything you do, realize He is there. That fact alone will help you direct your paths.

    Living the Christian life is simply living in the light of God's presence.

b) Unbelievers

    (1) Psalm 21:8—"Thine hand shall find out all thine enemies." An evil man has no hiding place from God.

    (2) Amos 9:2-4—"Though they dig into sheol, there shall mine hand take them; though they climb up to heaven, from there will I bring them down; and though they hide themselves in the top of Carmel, I will search and take them out from there; and though they be hidden from my sight in the bottom of the sea, there will I command the

serpent, and he shall bite them; and though they go into captivity before their enemies, there will I command the sword, and it shall slay them; and I will set mine eyes upon them for evil, and not for good."

(3) Obadiah 4—"Though thou exalt thyself like the eagle, and though thou set thy nest among the stars, from there will I bring thee down, saith the Lord." The ungodly must realize that no matter how they try to run from God or avoid thinking about Him, they cannot escape His attention.

(4) Job 34:21-22—"[God's] eyes are upon the ways of man, and he seeth all his goings. There is no darkness, nor shadow of death, where the workers of iniquity may hide themselves."

(5) Proverbs 15:11—"Sheol and destruction are before the Lord; how much more, then, the hearts of the children of men!" The thief steals because he thinks no one sees. The adulterer commits adultery because he thinks no one sees. The liar lies because he thinks he won't be caught. But God knows. Just because He is invisible doesn't mean He isn't present.

(6) Hebrews 4:13—"Neither is there any creature that is not manifest in his sight, but all things are naked and opened unto the eyes of him with whom we have to do."

(7) Isaiah 65:12—God said, "Ye . . . did evil before mine eyes."

(8) Proverbs 15:3—"The eyes of the Lord are in every place, beholding the evil and the good."

C. God Is All Powerful (Omnipotent)

1. The extent of God's power

   a) God can do anything

   There is nothing God can't do. There are no bounds to His energy. Job said, "If I speak of strength, lo, he is strong" (Job 9:19). One Hebrew name for God is *El Shaddai* (*El* refers to God; *Shaddai* means "almighty"). The psalmist said, "Power belongeth unto the Lord" (Ps. 62:11). And Revelation 19:6 says, "Halleluia! For the Lord God omnipotent reigneth."

   b) God can do anything effortlessly

   God can do one thing just as easily as He can do another. It is no more difficult for Him to create a universe than to make a butterfly. A. W. Tozer said, "Since He has at His command all the power in the universe, the Lord God omnipotent can do anything as easily as anything else. All His acts are done without effort. He expends no energy that must be replenished. His self-sufficiency makes it unnecessary for Him to look outside of Himself for a renewal of strength. All the power required to do all that He wills to do lies in undiminished fullness in His own infinite being" (*The Knowledge of the Holy*, p. 73). Isaiah 40:28 says the Lord "fainteth not, neither is weary."

   c) God can do anything He wants

   Psalm 115:3 says, "Our God is in the heavens; he hath done whatsoever he hath pleased." Although He can do anything according to His infinite ability and right, He will do only those things that are consistent with Himself. That's why He cannot lie, tolerate sin, save impenitent sinners, or punish innocent persons.

The Potter's Right

People often question what God does. They don't understand that He can do anything He wants. Romans 9 illustrates God's sovereignty in showing mercy on those He has elected (Isaac and Jacob), while hardening others (Esau and Pharaoh). To the one who argues with God's right to make those distinctions, Paul said, "Who are you, O man, who answers back to God? The thing molded will not say to the molder, 'Why did you make me like this,' will it? Or does not the potter have a right over the clay?" (vv. 20-21, NASB). Such power is frightening, but not as much when you remember that God is good.

2. The expression of God's power

   a) Creation

   Psalm 33:6 tells us that God spoke and the heavens were created. When we contemplate the power that exists in the created universe, or the power that man can generate through nuclear reactions, we have some idea of how great God's power is; it is greater than anything He ever made.

   No one helped God. In Isaiah 44:24 He says, "[I] stretcheth forth the heavens alone; who spreadeth abroad the earth by myself." He willed them into existence, and they did so the instant He willed it. Romans 4:17 says that God "calleth those things which are not, as though they were." Once He does, they are.

   b) Preservation

   He who made the world "upholds all things by the word of His power" (Heb. 1:3, NASB). A question often raised is, if God never gets tired, why did He rest on the seventh day of creation? But God didn't actually rest. If He had, everything He made on the first six days would have fallen apart. God doesn't get tired. God was just as active on the seventh day as He was the other six—upholding everything He had made.

   c) Redemption

   Redemption may be a greater display of God's power than creation. There apparently was no opposition to creation, but in redemption the devil had to be subdued, death had to be conquered, and sin had to be dealt with. Then God called to Himself a bunch of nobodies and caused them to confound the mighty (1 Cor. 1:26-27). God sent common people out into the world to spread the good news of His salvation. Within a short time they turned the world upside down (Acts 17:6).

d) Resurrection

God's power is visible in His ability to raise the dead. God has so much power that at the end of the age He will raise up from the dead every human being who has ever lived—both the righteous and unrighteous. John 5:28-29 says, "All that are in the graves shall hear his voice, and shall come forth: they that have done good, unto the resurrection of life; and they that have done evil, unto the resurrection of damnation." Revelation 20:11-15 refers to the Great White Throne of Judgment, where all the ungodly are brought before God.

3. The experience of God's power

a) By the believer

(1) The basis of our worship

Second Kings 17:36 says, "The Lord, who brought you up out of the land of Egypt with great power and an outstretched arm, him shall ye fear, and him shall ye worship." We are to worship God because of His power.

(2) The basis of daily confidence

Whenever you begin to feel inadequate, you need to turn to Philippians 4:13, where Paul says, "I can do all things through Christ, who strengtheneth me." Because of His power we can live confidently every day. Since we are "filled with all the fullness of God (Eph. 3:19), we are "able to do exceedingly abundantly above all that we ask or

think, according to the power that worketh in us"
(v. 20).

(3) The basis of resurrection hope

I look forward to being raised from the dead. The
only thing that would interfere with that plan
would be if I get raptured first. My confidence in
the resurrection is based on the power of God.
First Corinthians 15:20 says, "Now is Christ risen
from the dead and become the first fruits of them
that slept." Then verse 52 says, "In a moment, in
the twinkling of an eye, at the last trump; for the
trumpet shall sound, and the dead shall be raised
incorruptible, and we shall be changed." God
gives us victory over death (vv. 54-57).

(4) The basis of comfort

When you begin to worry about your problems,
realize there is nothing too great for God to handle. Psalm 121:1-2 says, "I will lift up mine eyes
unto the hills. From whence cometh my help? My
help cometh from the Lord, who made heaven
and earth." Since God made heaven and earth,
He can certainly handle any problem you have.

(5) The basis of victory

Ephesians 6:10 exhorts us to "be strong in the
Lord, and in the power of his might." In fighting
the enemy you need God's strength. You are like
a guard on watch. When the adversary comes,
you're not supposed to fight him yourself—you
tell the commander and he leads the battle. God
can bring about the victory because "greater is he
that is in you, than he that is in the world" (1
John 4:4). Satan is a powerful enemy, but you can
handle him because the victory is yours in Christ
(1 John 3:8).

(6) The basis of assurance

Now that you are saved, you will remain saved because God is powerful enough to keep you saved. The only way you could be removed from God's protective hand would be if someone more powerful than Him took you away. But there isn't anyone more powerful than God.

(*a*) John 10:28-29—Jesus said of those who would follow Him, "I give unto them eternal life, and they shall never perish, neither shall any man pluck them out of my hand. My Father, who gave them to me, is greater than all, and no man is able to pluck them out of my Father's hand."

(*b*) Romans 8:33, 35, 38-39—"Who shall lay any thing to the charge of God's elect? . . . What shall separate us from the love of Christ? . . . Neither death, nor life, nor angels, nor principalities, nor powers, nor things present, nor things to come, nor height, nor depth, nor any other creation, shall be able to separate us from the love of God, which is in Christ Jesus, our Lord."

(*c*) 2 Timothy 1:12—Paul said, "I am not ashamed; for I know whom I have believed and am persuaded that he is able to keep that which I have committed unto him against that day."

(7) The basis of humility

It's easy to be proud if your thoughts aren't on God but on yourself. First Peter 5:6 says, "Humble yourselves, therefore, under the mighty hand of God, that he may exalt you in due time." Apart from God's power you can accomplish nothing.

b) By the unbeliever

   (1) 1 Corinthians 10:22—Paul asked the rhetorical question, "Do we provoke the Lord to jealousy? Are we stronger than he?" Since God becomes jealous when people don't worship Him, He will reveal His wrath against them (Rom. 1:18). A tragic future is in store for people who don't know God or Christ. The omnipotent God will ultimately confront them in judgment. And unless they are stronger than He, they have no defense. But of course, no man is stronger than God, who is his Creator.

   (2) Job 9:4—"He is wise in heart, and mighty in strength. Who hath hardened himself against him, and hath prospered?" The obvious answer is, no one.

   (3) 2 Thessalonians 1:7-9—"The Lord Jesus shall be revealed from heaven with his mighty angels, in flaming fire taking vengeance on them that know not God, and that obey not the gospel of our Lord Jesus Christ; who shall be punished with everlasting destruction from the presence of the Lord, and from the glory of his power."

   (4) Hebrews 10:31—"It is a fearful thing to fall into the hands of the living God."

Conclusion

God's attributes create two different responses, depending on one's relationship to Him. To know that God is unchangeable, omnipresent, and all powerful brings joy to the Christian. But the same attributes cause fear in the unbeliever. The issue isn't God's character; it's man's response to Him.

God desires worship. In Jeremiah 14:16 God promises punishment for those who don't come to Him. Yet in verse 17 He says, "Mine eyes run down with tears night and day." God is grieved because He loves sinners. When a sinner repents and accepts the sacrifice of Christ on his behalf, God joyfully accepts him. Then, instead of God's attributes causing fear, they cause joy.

Focusing on the Facts

1. According to A. W. Tozer, what is the most important message the church has to offer (see p. 29)?
2. What is the essence of idolatry (see pp. 29-30)?
3. Why shouldn't we allow comparisons from the human realm to determine God's character (see p. 30)?
4. Briefly explain the nature of God's omnipresence (see p. 31).
5. What have been some common misconceptions about God's presence (see pp. 31-32)?
6. What does 1 John 3:5 and Jesus' interaction with sinners illustrate about God (see p. 32)?
7. How does God's relational presence differ from His essential presence (see p. 33)?
8. Name some of the symbolic representations of God's majesty (see p. 33).
9. In what ways do believers benefit from God's omnipresence? Explain each one (see pp. 34-36).
10. What should God's omnipresence clearly reveal to the unbeliever (see pp. 36-37)?
11. Briefly explain God's omnipotence (see pp. 37-38).
12. Explain what is meant by the effortlessness of God's power (see p. 38).
13. In what ways do believers experience God's power? Explain each one (see pp. 40-42).
14. What does God's omnipotence mean to an unbeliever (see p. 43)?

Pondering the Principles

1. Perhaps one of the greatest applications of God's omnipresence is its motivation to holiness. When you have deliberately sinned against God's revealed will, what clouded your thinking? Did you rationalize your sin by supposing that God wouldn't judge

your sin or that He didn't see your sin? We must allow God's presence to motivate us to lead holy lives. Read 1 Corinthians 6:9-20 and list what God has done and the resulting principles that flow out of what He has done. For example, verse 11 declares what God has done to give us freedom, but verses 12-13 exhort us to limit that freedom.

2. The next time you need comfort, meditate on God's promise never to leave you or forsake you (Heb. 13:5). Also reflect on God's power (see Eph. 3:19-20). Rest in the confidence that God knows your situation and provides His strength so that you can endure it for your spiritual growth and His glory (see Rom. 8:28-29; 1 Cor. 10:13; 1 Pet. 5:10-11).

3
God—Part 3

Outline

Introduction
A. Man's Highest Pursuit
   1. Proverbs 9:10
   2. John 17:3
   3. 1 Chronicles 28:9
   4. 2 Peter 3:18
   5. 2 Thessalonians 1:8
B. God's Highest Purpose

Review
I. God—Is He?
II. God—Who Is He?
III. God—What Is He Like?
A. God Is Unchanging (Immutable)
B. God Is Everywhere (Omnipresent)
C. God Is All Powerful (Omnipotent)

Lesson
D. God Knows Everything (Omniscient)
   1. The extent of God's omniscience
      a) In general
         (1) God is infinite
         (2) God is wise
         (3) God is authoritative
      b) Toward men
         (1) God's continuing love for us
         (2) God's detailed knowledge about us
            (*a*) The external
            (*b*) The internal

     i) Revelation 2:23
     ii) Psalm 139:12
     iii) Psalm 139:4
     iv) Isaiah 66:18
     v) John 2:24-25
  2. The revelation of God's omniscience
    a) His wisdom in creation
    b) His wisdom in providence
    c) His wisdom in redemption
  3. The application of God's omniscience
    a) To the believer
     (1) Comfort
      (*a*) Malachi 3:16-17
      (*b*) Psalm 56:8
      (*c*) Matthew 6:25-33
     (2) Confidence
     (3) Correction
    b) To the unbeliever
     (1) The futility of hypocrisy
     (2) The foundation of judgment
      (*a*) Romans 2:2
      (*b*) Jeremiah 16:17
     (3) The folly of human wisdom
E. God Is Without Sin (Holy)
  1. The proclamation of God's holiness
    a) Exodus 15:11
    b) Psalm 111:9
    c) Job 6:10
    d) Isaiah 6:3
    e) 1 Samuel 2:2
  2. The pursuit of God's holiness
    a) Confessing sin
    b) Acknowledging the standard
    c) Believing in Christ
  3. The perspectives on God's holiness
    a) His hatred of sin
     (1) Habakkuk 1:13
     (2) Amos 5:21-23
    b) His love for the sinner
  4. The portrayal of God's holiness
    a) In creation
    b) In the moral law
    c) In the sacrificial law

d) In His judgment on sin
e) In the death of Christ
5. The practicality of God's holiness
   a) For the unbeliever
   b) For the believer
      (1) It distinguishes us from the world
      (2) It gives us boldness before God
      (3) It gives us peace

Introduction

A. Man's Highest Pursuit

To know God and all that He has revealed about Himself is the highest pursuit in life.

1. Proverbs 9:10—"The fear of the Lord is the beginning of wisdom, and the knowledge of the Holy One is understanding."

2. John 17:3—"This is eternal life, that they might know thee, the only true God, and Jesus Christ, whom thou hast sent." Knowing God is synonymous with eternal life. Eternal life is knowing God intimately for all eternity by partaking of His very nature (2 Pet. 1:4).

3. 1 Chronicles 28:9—David gave the following advice: "Solomon, my son, know thou the God of thy father, and serve him with a perfect heart and with a willing mind; for the Lord searcheth all hearts, and understandeth all the imaginations of the thoughts. If thou seek him, he will be found by thee; but if thou forsake him, he will cast thee off forever."

4. 2 Peter 3:18—"Grow in grace, and in the knowledge of our Lord and Savior, Jesus Christ."

5. 2 Thessalonians 1:8—Jesus will return "in flaming fire taking vengeance on them that know not God."

B. God's Highest Purpose

It is a serious matter when those who claim to know God don't. Through the prophet Hosea, God rebuked the people of Israel for performing the prescribed sacrifices with hearts totally estranged from Him. In Hosea 6:6 He says, "I desired mercy, and not sacrifice, and the knowledge of God more than burnt offerings." More than any other thing, God desires that we know Him.

How Can We Know God?

1. Jeremiah 29:13—"Ye shall seek me, and find me, when ye shall search for me with all your heart."

2. Proverbs 2:3-5—Solomon said, "If thou criest after knowledge, and liftest up thy voice for understanding; if thou seekest her as silver, and searchest for her as for hidden treasures; then shalt thou understand the fear of the Lord, and find the knowledge of God." There is only one way to know God and that is to make knowing Him your life's pursuit. If you seek only money or success, you'll be distracted from discovering all there is to know about God.

Review

Lesson

D. God Knows Everything (Omniscient)

1. The extent of God's omniscience

   a) In general

   (1) God is infinite

   Psalm 147:5 says God's "understanding is infinite." That means it is limitless. First Samuel 2:3 says that "the Lord is a God of knowledge." The Hebrew word translated "knowledge" is plural. That intensifies the fact that God's great knowledge is vastly beyond ours.

   (2) God is wise

   First Timothy 1:17 identifies God as "the only wise God" (cf. Rom. 16:27; Jude 25). Only He knows what He knows. The angels know a lot, and we know some things, but no one knows as much as God. His infinite wisdom and knowledge is unrivaled.

   (3) God is authoritative

   God never needs to learn anything. When you pray, you're not telling God anything He doesn't already know. He just wants you to line up your desires with His will, and that's why He chooses to work through your prayers. There are no surprises for Him. Isaiah 40:13 says, "Who hath directed the Spirit of the Lord, or being his counselor, taught him?" Romans 11:34 says: "Who hath known the mind of the Lord? Or who hath been his counselor?" Who taught God? No one.

b) Toward men

(1) God's continuing love for us

Perhaps the most astounding fact about God's omniscience is that even though He knows all about us, we're still here. He loves us in spite of our sin. Isaiah 48:8-11 illustrates God's gracious and merciful love: "Thou heardest not; yea, thou knewest not; yea, from that time thine ear was not opened; for I knew that thou wouldest deal very treacherously, and wast called a transgressor from the womb. For my name's sake will I defer mine anger, and for my praise will I refrain for thee, that I cut thee not off. Behold, I have refined thee, but not with silver; I have chosen thee in the furnace of affliction. For mine own sake, even for mine own sake, will I do it." In spite of their rebelliousness, God faithfully guaranteed Israel's undeserved redemption. The salvation of sinners displays God's love to the world (1 John 4:9-10) and His wisdom to the angels (Eph. 3:10).

(2) God's detailed knowledge about us

Nothing is hidden from God.

(*a*) The external

Luke 12:7 says, "Even the very hairs of your head are all numbered." God doesn't need to count the hairs on your head—He just knows how many there are.

(*b*) The internal

i) Revelation 2:23—Christ "searcheth the minds and hearts." He sees our heart and mind just as well as the external characteristics of our bodies.

ii) Psalm 139:12—The darkness of night is no canopy to God because "the darkness hideth not from [Him]." John 3:19 says, "Men loved darkness rather than light, because their deeds were evil." Though men try to hide their sin, the brilliant light of God's omniscience exposes it.

iii) Psalm 139:4—"There is not a word in my tongue, but, lo, O Lord, thou knowest it altogether." God hears your whispers as if they were broadcast.

iv) Isaiah 66:18—Not one of your thoughts is outside the knowledge of God: "I know their works and their thoughts."

v) John 2:24-25—Jesus "knew all men, and needed not that any should testify of man; for he knew what was in man." For example, when Nicodemus asked Jesus a question, Jesus answered the real question he had in mind (John 3:1-4).

There isn't a secret place in your house or anywhere else where you can hide from God. And you can be confident that that is accurate because Deuteronomy 32:4 calls Him "a God of truth," and Titus 1:2 says He "cannot lie."

The Divine Lay-Away Plan

Hosea 13:12 says, "The iniquity of Ephraim is bound up; his sin is hidden." People look at that verse and hope there are some sins God doesn't know about. But that is not the case. The Bible is clear on the fact that God knows everything. Hosea 13:12, rather than contradicting God's omniscience, is saying that the Northern Kingdom's rebellion was being put away for a future day of judgment. You might call it the divine lay-away plan—sin now, pay later.

Often it appears that godly people are under more stress than the ungodly. Though many ungodly people prosper now (Ps. 37:1-2, 9-20), they won't always prosper. Perhaps like Ephraim their sin is hidden for now, waiting for the day of judgment in the future. In

Romans 2:5-6 Paul says, "After thy hardness and impenitent heart treasurest up unto thyself wrath against the day of wrath and revelation of the righteous judgment of God, who will render to every man according to his deeds." There will come a day when the sin that is now hidden will be unmasked and punished.

2. The revelation of God's omniscience

Closely related to God's omniscience is His wisdom. His wisdom could be defined as His omniscience acting with a holy will. Since God knows everything, everything He does is absolutely wise. He knows the beginning, the end, and every step in between. God has perfect knowledge, which results in perfect wisdom (or practical omniscience).

a) His wisdom in creation

You can see God's wisdom in everything—from the macrocosm of the universe to the microcosm of life. God formed the entire universe out of innumerable component parts. And each part functions in harmony with every other part, resulting in exactly what God intended. God's creation is a monument to His wisdom. Psalm 104:24 says, "O Lord, how manifold are thy works! In wisdom hast thou made them all."

b) His wisdom in providence

Ephesians 1:11 tells us that God "worketh all things after the counsel of his own will."

c) His wisdom in redemption

God called people who weren't wise, mighty, or noble to be His people (1 Cor. 1:26). Ephesians 3:10 tells us that God put the redeemed church on display before angels that they might see God's wisdom.

3. The application of God's omniscience

   a) To the believer

      (1) Comfort

      It is comforting to know that God knows everything. In the vastness of this universe you're assured that you are not insignificant—God knows you personally.

      (a) Malachi 3:16-17—In Malachi's day a small remnant of God's faithful feared that He would forget them and judge them with the rest of the people: "They that feared the Lord spoke often one to another; and the Lord hearkened, and heard it, and a book of remembrance was written before him for them that feared the Lord, and that thought upon his name. And they shall be mine, saith the Lord of hosts, in that day when I make up my jewels; and I will spare them, as a man spareth his own son that serveth him." God has a book and He doesn't forget who's in it. He knows those who belong to Jesus Christ. He put their names in the Book of Life before the world began (Eph. 1:4).

      (b) Psalm 56:8—"Thou numberest my wanderings; put thou my tears into thy bottle." It was a common practice in the Orient to hire mourners for funerals. Those mourners would catch their tears in a bottle. Perhaps that was how they proved they performed their task. David's statement that God catches our tears tells us that He knows why we have them. He knows us, and He knows every trial we have to endure.

      (c) Matthew 6:25-33—Jesus said, "Be not anxious for your life, what ye shall eat, or what ye shall drink; nor yet for your body, what ye shall put on. Is not the life more than food and the body than raiment? Behold the fowls of the air; for they sow not, neither do they reap, nor gather into barns, yet your heavenly Father feedeth them. Are ye not much better than they? Which of you by being anxious can add one cubit unto his stature? And why are ye anxious for raiment? Consider the lilies of the field, how they grow; they toil not, neither do they spin, and yet I say unto you that even Solomon, in all his glory, was not arrayed like one of these. Wherefore, if God so clothe the grass of the field, which today is, and tomorrow is cast into the oven, shall he not much more clothe you, O ye of little faith? Therefore, be not anxious saying, What shall we eat? or, What shall we drink? or, With what shall we be clothed? For after all these things do the Gentiles seek. For your heavenly Father knoweth that ye have need of all these things. But seek ye first the kingdom of God, and his righteousness, and all these things shall be added unto you."

God knows your needs and takes care of them all. In the midst of His care He never makes a mistake. When you take into account God's infinite attributes and knowledge, you have no basis for ever accusing God of making a mistake. Just realize you don't know that much, and accept whatever God does as perfect.

(2) Confidence

When I was a child I pictured the doctrine of omniscience as anything but confidence-inspiring; my parents were often reminding me that God knew everything I did. But as I grew up, I began to realize that God's omniscience is truly a benefit for the Christian. After twice trying to convince the Lord that he loved Him, Peter said, "Lord, thou knowest all things; thou knowest that I love thee" (John 21:17). Peter appealed to Christ's omniscience. If it weren't for His omniscience, God would be perfectly justified in questioning our love for Him.

(3) Correction

If you thought God didn't know everything and would never find out what you did, what would you feel free to do that you're not doing now? If you want to know where your sinful flesh is the strongest, imagine what you would do if you knew He wouldn't find out. But He does know. Fortunately He is one teacher who never leaves the room. And we can be thankful that His correction is always done in love (Heb. 12:6). In the same way that God's omnipresence is a deterrent to sin, so is His omniscience. Every sin is committed in God's presence and in His knowledge.

b) To the unbeliever

(1) The futility of hypocrisy

Unbelievers can't play games with God because He knows everything. All hypocrisy is unmasked before Him. In the Sermon on the Mount Jesus confronted the religious hypocrisy of the day and tore the masks off the self-righteous. In Ecclesiastes 12:14 Solomon says, "God shall bring every work into judgment, with every secret thing, whether it be good, or whether it be evil." God sees through every hypocritical front. First Samuel 16:7 reminds us that "the Lord seeth not as a man seeth; for man looketh on the outward appearance, but the Lord looketh on the heart."

(2) The foundation of judgment

God will be just and accurate in His judgment.

(a) Romans 2:2—Paul said, "We are sure that the judgment of God is according to truth." The judgment that determines who will be sent to hell for all eternity will be just, because God, who has absolute knowledge of truth, will judge on the basis of truth. And no one can fool God.

(b) Jeremiah 16:17—God said, "Their iniquity [is not] hidden from mine eyes." There is no way anyone can hide from the truthful judgment of God. He knows whose sin remains unforgiven. He knows who has put up a facade of religiosity. He knows whose name is in the Book of Life and whose isn't.

(3) The folly of human wisdom

Since God knows everything, those who are truly wise will learn from His knowledge. Solomon continually counseled his son to seek knowledge (Prov. 8:1-36). A foolish man pursues the knowledge of the world (Prov. 17:24). In 1 Corinthians 1:19 God says, "I will destroy the wisdom of the wise, and will bring to nothing the understanding of the prudent."

E. God Is Without Sin (Holy)

1. The proclamation of God's holiness

Holiness is arguably the most significant of all God's attributes. God is holy. When the angels sing in heaven they don't say, "Eternal, eternal, eternal"; "Faithful, faithful, faithful"; "Wise, wise, wise"; or "Mighty, mighty, mighty." But they do sing, "Holy, holy, holy, Lord God Almighty" (Rev. 4:8).

a) Exodus 15:11—"Who is like thee, glorious in holiness, fearful in praise, doing wonders?" The answer obviously is no one.

b) Psalm 111:9—"Holy and reverend is his name."

c) Job 6:10—Job referred to God as "the Holy One."

d) Isaiah 6:3—The angels said, "Holy, holy, holy, is the Lord of hosts; the whole earth is full of his glory."

e) 1 Samuel 2:2—"There is none holy like the Lord; for there is none beside thee."

2. The pursuit of God's holiness

Perhaps the best way to understand God's holiness is to compare it to sin.

a) Confessing sin

One of the most revealing passages regarding God's holiness is Isaiah 6. Isaiah said, "In the year that King Uzziah died, I saw also the Lord sitting upon a throne, high and lifted up, and his train filled the temple. Above it stood the seraphim: each one had six wings; with two he covered his face, and with two he covered his feet, and with two he did fly. . . . Then said I, Woe is me! For I am undone, because I am a man of unclean lips; for mine eyes have seen the King" (vv. 1-2, 5). Isaiah was shaken to the core of his being. Why? Because he had seen the holiness of God in contrast to his own sinfulness. An understanding of both your sin and God's holiness is necessary. You'll never recognize your sin until you understand God's holiness, yet you can't know His holiness until you see your sin. Once Isaiah saw God in His exalted state, he saw himself for what he was and then poured out his heart to God.

b) Acknowledging the standard

Between you and God is a gulf separating holiness from unholiness. You are unholy; He is holy. As a result you ought to be shaken to the roots of your being when you see yourself in comparison to His holiness.

God doesn't conform to some holy standard—He is the standard. He never does anything wrong. He never misjudges anything. He never makes a mistake. There are no degrees to His holiness—He is perfectly holy. Consequently, holiness is the standard for existing in His presence. When some of the angels sinned, God immediately separated them from His presence (2 Pet. 2:4). Similarly when men and women reject Jesus Christ, they are sent "into everlasting fire, prepared for the devil and his angels" (Matt. 25:41).

c) Believing in Christ

How can we be holy? By exercising faith in the Lord Jesus Christ. Through Christ's atoning work on the cross, God imputes holiness to those who believe in Him (2 Cor. 5:21). Paul said to the Corinthians, "You were washed, you were sanctified, you were justified in the name of the Lord Jesus" (1 Cor. 6:11, NIV*).

3. The perspectives on God's holiness

a) His hatred of sin

A good way to understand God's holiness is to see it in contrast to His hatred of sin. We can much more easily understand His hatred of sin than His holiness, since we are so familiar with sin.

(1) Habakkuk 1:13—"Thou art of purer eyes than to behold evil, and canst not look on iniquity."

(2) Amos 5:21-23—God said, "I hate, I despise your feast days, and I will not take delight in your solemn assemblies. Though ye offer me burnt offerings and your meal offerings, I will not accept them; neither will I regard the peace offerings of your fat beasts. Take away from me the noise of thy songs; for I will not hear the melody of thine harps." God had instituted ceremonial and sacrificial ordinances for the people to follow, but they performed them with impure hearts. God hates that. He doesn't want people doing right things with the wrong attitude. Sin is the object of His displeasure, but He loves holiness. Psalm 11:7 says, "The righteous Lord loveth righteousness."

b) His love for the sinner

Although God is holy and hates sin, He still redeemed us. He knows us and despises our sin, yet He loves us. God's holiness, omniscience, and love

* *New International Version*

all act in harmony. To better understand that kind of love, consider what it might be like to have cancer. Even though your body would be infected with cancer, you would love your body but hate the cancer. You would do everything you could to preserve your body—to keep it healthy and strong and to minister to its needs. And you would do everything you could to destroy the cancer. Similarly God loves man but despises his sin.

God never wills for anyone to sin. He gives us freedom of choice, and we so often choose to sin, but He never wills it. He also never tempts anyone to sin (James 1:13-14).

4. The portrayal of God's holiness

   a) In creation

   Ecclesiastes 7:29 says, "God hath made man upright; but they have sought out many devices." God made man holy.

   b) In the moral law

   God's moral law still pervades the world although man has tried to pervert it. Romans 7:12 says, "The law is holy, and the commandment is holy, and just, and good." God's moral law proves that He is righteous, moral, and holy.

   c) In the sacrificial law

   When God instructed the Israelites to offer animals as a sacrifice for sin, He was telling them that death is the result of sin. It also communicated that God cannot be approached without a substitutionary sacrifice for sin (Heb. 9:22).

   d) In His judgment on sin

   Second Thessalonians 1:7-8 says, "The Lord Jesus shall be revealed from heaven with his mighty angels, in flaming fire taking vengeance on them that know not God, and that obey not the gospel." Jude 15 says that the Lord will come "to execute judgment upon all, and to convict all that are ungodly among them of all their ungodly deeds which they have ungodly committed, and of all their hard speeches which ungodly sinners have spoken against him." God's judgment on sin is a reflection of His holiness because He must punish it.

e) In the death of Christ

Perhaps the greatest expression of God's holiness was His sending His Son to die on a cross (Rom. 8:3). God was so holy that He paid the highest price necessary to satisfy His holiness. Hebrews 9:26 says, "For then must he often have suffered since the foundation of the world." That means that if Christ had to continually make an offering for sin as the Old Testament priests had to do, He would have to die over and over again. But verse 26 says, "Now once, in the end of the ages, hath he appeared to put away sin by the sacrifice of himself." God's holiness is so infinite that He had to pay the supreme price of bearing sin and dying a sacrificial death.

5. The practicality of God's holiness

a) For the unbeliever

The holiness of God demands holiness in everyone, and that can be accomplished only through Jesus Christ. Hebrews 12:14 says that without holiness "no man shall see the Lord." Ephesians 4:24 says to "put on the new man, which after God is created in righteousness and true holiness." The only way to accommodate God's demand for holiness is to accept Christ and receive His righteousness. But to reject the holiness God offers in Jesus Christ is to activate God's justice. The impenitent sinner will receive what he deserves.

b) For the believer

First Peter 1:15-16 gives us the practical implication of God's holiness for us: "As he who hath called you is holy, so be ye holy in all manner of life, because it is written, Be ye holy; for I am holy." Since God is holy, He wants His people to be holy.

(1) It distinguishes us from the world

Positionally we are holy in Christ, but God wants our practical lives to match our position. He wants us to live holy lives. The world needs to see the difference that knowing Christ makes. Second Timothy 2:19 says, "Let every one that nameth the name of Christ depart from iniquity." If you're going to claim to follow Christ, then live a life that proves you do.

(2) It gives us boldness before God

If you're living a holy life and regularly confessing and repenting of sin in your life, you will have boldness before God. Job 22:23-26 says, "If thou return to the Almighty, thou shalt be built up; thou shalt put away iniquity very far from thy tents. . . . Then shalt thou have thy delight in the Almighty, and shall lift up thy face unto God." You can't face God and delight in Him when there's sin in your life. Whenever there is sin, you are liable to discover what I have discovered: you'll have a difficult time praying.

(3) It gives us peace

Isaiah 57:21 says, "There is no peace, saith my God, to the wicked."

God wants us holy even if He has to chastise us (Heb. 12:10). What should a Christian do to become holy? What David did in Psalm 51:9-10: pray for a clean heart. Then we should heed the instruction of Proverbs 13:20 to be around those who will influence us toward holiness.

Focusing on the Facts

1. What is the highest pursuit in life (see p. 49)?
2. What is God's greatest desire (see p. 50)?
3. What does God promise to those who seek Him (Jer. 29:13; see p. 50)?
4. Define God's omniscience (see p. 51).
5. Although God knows we are sinners, what is His attitude toward us (see p. 52)?
6. What two things does the salvation of sinners display (Eph. 3:10; 1 John 4:9-10; see p. 52)?
7. What does God know about us? Be specific (see pp. 52-53).
8. Explain God's divine lay-away plan (see pp. 53-54).
9. In what way is God's wisdom closely related to His omniscience (see p. 54)?
10. How is God's wisdom revealed (see p. 54)?
11. In what ways can believers apply God's omniscience to their lives? Explain each one (see pp. 55-57).
12. What should God's omniscience reveal to an unbeliever about hypocrisy, judgment, and human wisdom (see pp. 57-58)?
13. What must anyone come to grips with before he can begin to understand God's holiness (see p. 59)?
14. What is the standard for anyone to be able to exist in God's presence (see p. 59)?
15. How can unholy man be declared holy (2 Cor. 5:21; see p. 60)?
16. Explain the balance between God's hatred of sin and His love for sinners (see pp. 60-61).
17. In what ways is God's holiness revealed (see pp. 61-62)?
18. What is perhaps the greatest expression of God's holiness (see p. 62)?
19. What is the consequence of rejecting the holiness God offers (see p. 62)?
20. What are some practical ways in which a Christian can apply God's holiness (see p. 63)?

Pondering the Principles

1. Do you trust God to meet all your needs? That is easier said than done, especially when faced with difficult trials. Yet know that God knows your needs no matter what your circumstances may

be, and He promises to meet them. According to Matthew 6:33, what is the believer's first responsibility? Read Philippians 4:6, 11-13. What are we commanded to do? What attitude did Paul exemplify that we should imitate? Begin to put those principles into practice in your life.

2. Before we can pursue holiness, we must truly desire it, knowing that God desires us to be holy. Read 1 Peter 1:13–2:3 and list as many reasons as you can to live a holy life. As Christians, we are in the world but not of it (1 Cor. 5:9-10), yet we still can be negatively influenced by it. For that reason Psalm 1:1 cautions us not to allow the world's system to direct our lives. Verse 2 tells us that God's Word should be our guide. Read Romans 10:17 and 1 John 5:4-5. What is the key to victory over the world's system? What preventative steps can you take to counteract those things in your life that are hindering your spiritual growth toward being Christlike?

4
Satan—Part 1

Outline

Introduction
A. A Critical Strategy
B. A Cursory Study
   1. The revelation about angels
     a) Job 38:4-7
     b) Colossians 1:16
   2. The responsibility of angels
   3. The rebellion of angels
     a) The incomprehensibility of the rebellion
     b) The leader of the rebellion

Lesson
I. Satan—Is He?
  A. The Philosophical Evidence
   1. The dichotomy
   2. The denial
   3. The defense
  B. The Biblical Evidence
   1. The acknowledgment of Satan
     a) By Jesus
       (1) Matthew 4:1-4
       (2) John 12:31
       (3) John 14:30
       (4) John 16:11
       (5) John 8:44
     b) By Paul
     c) By John
     d) By James
     e) By Peter

2. The activity of Satan
   a) He tempted Eve (Gen. 3:1-6)
   b) He tempted Christ (Matt. 4:1-11)
   c) He perverts God's Word (Gen. 3:1; Matt. 4:6)
   d) He opposes God's work (Zech. 3:1)
   e) He hinders God's servants (1 Thess. 2:18)
   f) He hinders the gospel (Matt. 13:19, 38-39; 2 Cor. 4:4)
   g) He ensnares the wicked (1 Tim. 3:7; 2 Tim. 2:26)
   h) He deceives the nations (1 Kings 22:6-7, 19-23; Rev. 16:14; 20:7-8)
   i) He disguises himself as an angel of light (2 Cor. 11:3, 14)
   j) He contended with the angel Michael (Jude 9)
   k) He instigated the fall of the human race (Gen. 3:13-24)
   l) He seeks to devour (1 Pet. 5:8)
   m) He accuses God's people (Job 1:6-12; 2:1-6; Rev. 12:10)
   n) He once had the power of death (Heb. 2:14)
   o) The whole world lies in his power (1 John 5:19)
   C. The Experiential Evidence
II. Satan—Who Is He?
   A. He Is a Person
      1. His traits
         a) The ability to plan
         b) The ability to communicate
         c) The ability to will something
      2. His accountability
      3. His names
         a) The anointed cherub (Ezek. 28:14)
         b) The prince of this world (John 16:11)
         c) The prince of the power of the air (Eph. 2:2)
         d) The god of this age (2 Cor. 4:4)
         e) Beelzebub, the chief of demons (Luke 11:15)
   B. He Is a Spirit
      1. His immaterial composition
      2. His spatial limitation
      3. His visual manifestation
      4. His immortal status
   C. He Is a Fallen Angel
      1. Satan's rise and fall (Ezekiel 28)
         a) His beauty
         b) His preexistence

c) His talent
   d) His position
   e) His sin
2. Satan's pride and punishment (Isaiah 14)
   a) The expression of his pride
      (1) "I will ascend into heaven" (v. 13a)
      (2) "I will exalt my throne above the stars of God"
          (v. 13b)
      (3) "I will sit also upon the mount of the congrega-
          tion [assembly]" (v. 13c)
      (4) "I will ascend above the heights of the clouds"
          (v. 14a)
      (5) "I will be like the Most High [Heb., *elyon*]"
          (v. 14b)
   b) The execution of his punishment

Conclusion
A. The Reality of Spiritual Conflict
B. The Response to Christ's Call

Introduction

A. A Critical Strategy

When I played football in college, one thing the coaches often did was to use the third- or fourth-string units to run
plays similar to those of the team we would face in our
game on Saturday. They would practice against the first-
and second-string units so the latter could get a better idea
of what to expect from their opponent. Being able to pre-
dict what your enemy will do is very important, and that
principle is no less true in the spiritual realm. If we want to
gain victory in spiritual things, we need to know our enemy. The better we understand him, the better we will recognize his weaknesses. Only then does he become vulnerable to us. That's why it's important to do a study on Satan.
We certainly don't intend to glorify him. But we do need to
unmask him so that we can see him as he is—a corrupt and
defeated being.

B. A Cursory Study

1. The revelation about angels

Genesis 1:1-2 says, "In the beginning God created the heaven and the earth. And the earth was without form, and void; and darkness was upon the face of the deep. And the Spirit of God moved upon the face of the waters." That's the account of creation with which we are all familiar. Yet that was not the first creation. Elsewhere Scripture tells us that at that time, there were already created beings in existence.

a) Job 38:4-7—God rhetorically asked Job, "Where wast thou when I laid the foundations of the earth? Declare, if thou hast understanding" (v. 4). That is an obvious reference to the Genesis creation. The Lord continued, "Who hath laid the measures of it, if thou knowest? Or who hath stretched the line upon it? Whereupon are its foundations fastened? Or who laid its cornerstone, when the morning stars sang together, and all the sons of God shouted for joy?" (vv. 5-7)

"The morning stars" and "the sons of God" existed before the creation of the universe. Since "morning stars" is here used synonymously with "sons of God [Heb. *bene Elohim*]," a clear reference to angels (Job 1:6; 2:1), we assume it, too, refers to angels. It obviously isn't a reference to literal stars since the universe hadn't been created yet. We don't know when angels were created, but it's safe to conclude that they were in existence before the universe was made.

b) Colossians 1:16—Paul said of Christ, "By him were all things created, that are in heaven, and that are in earth, visible and invisible, whether they be thrones, or dominions, or principalities, or powers—all things were created by him, and for him." The Greek words translated "thrones," "dominions," "principalities," and "powers" are titles for angels and signify their ranking. The Greek verb translated "were created" is in the aorist tense implying that all

70

the angels had been created at the same time by a direct act of God in the past.

2. The responsibility of angels

Angels were created to serve and glorify God. Revelation 4 shows the angels glorifying God with their praise. Hebrews 1:14 calls them "ministering spirits." Angels serve the purposes of God by carrying out His bidding and offering Him praise.

3. The rebellion of angels

At some point between their creation and Genesis 3, something happened to some of the angels. One is seen as an evil serpent in the Garden (Gen. 3:1). A tragedy had occurred: a large group of angels had rebelled against their Creator (Rev. 12:9). They are known as demons.

a) The incomprehensibility of the rebellion

One of the most difficult questions in all theology is the problem of theodicy, which is the defense of God's goodness in view of the existence of evil. Where did sin come from? It apparently originated with the angels since they sinned first. That's about all we can deduce from the scriptural evidence. For His own reasons, God did not choose to reveal everything to us (Deut. 29:29).

Why would angels want to rebel against an absolutely holy God? They are intelligent beings; they must have recognized that they had a glorious existence. They had the ability to communicate with God. Their emotional makeup is seen in their praising God. They were responsible creatures. They weren't robots; they had wills as evidenced by their choice to rebel. We don't know why they did it or how. We don't know how that temptation manifested itself in Lucifer's mind (Ezek. 28:15), but we know that mankind's present sinful condition is a result of that rebellion.

71

b) The leader of the rebellion

In Matthew 25:41 our Lord refers to "the devil and his angels." Satan led a group of angels in rebellion against God. How many angels followed him? Revelation 12:3 refers to Satan as the great red dragon. Verse 4 says, "His tail drew the third part of the stars of heaven and did cast them to earth." Since "stars" in Job 38:7 refers to angels, Revelation 12:4 apparently means that one-third of the angels rebelled with Satan.

Lesson

I. SATAN—IS HE?

Some people scoff at the devil's existence, assuming he is nothing more than an evil character contrived to scare kids on Halloween. Is there any evidence that supports the existence of a devil—a personal, active being who is opposed to the plan of God?

A. The Philosophical Evidence

1. The dichotomy

From a philosophical perspective we can conclude that there must be an adversary, because absolute harmony does not exist in the world. We know that God was powerful enough to create a perfect world. Yet there exists a puzzling dichotomy of happiness and sorrow, of wisdom and stupidity, of fulfillment and failure, of kindness and cruelty, of life and death. Something or someone evil has obviously messed with perfection.

2. The denial

That opposition to God exists is evidence of some other personal being actively engaged in trying to stifle God's plans. Is it logical to assume that God would create good and then create its opposite—evil—to fight against His efforts? No. That's like asking, "Can God make a rock so big He can't lift it?" In *The King of the Earth* Erich Sauer quotes Dr. von Gerdteil as saying, "On the one hand it [the universe] shows too much intelligence, wisdom and happiness to justify a denial of God; on the other hand it shows too much lack of intelligence, malignity and unhappiness to make belief in God probable. It gives the impression of a magnificent temple in ruins in which its inscriptions expressing profound truth have been maliciously and skilfully caricatured by some unknown person" ([Grand Rapids: Eerdmans, 1962], p. 61).

3. The defense

Sauer himself said, "The existence of sorrow and evil throughout the world proves the existence of a transcendental, real, dynamic, hostile power, not willed by God" (p. 62). God wouldn't create something perfect and then stand in opposition to it. Sauer then said, "The fact is that the devil is a spiritual being . . . whose existence cannot in any way be assailed by philosophy nor natural science. Since it is just in our world and in our universe immediately surrounding us that we observe disharmony, death, and destruction, even a purely speculative contemplation of nature focuses on us the conclusion that this world, and presumably the solar system connected with it, are the domain of this world-ruler and potentate" (p. 63). Obviously a being exists who fights the purposes of God.

B. The Biblical Evidence

1. The acknowledgment of Satan

   a) By Jesus

   Christ obviously believed that the devil exists.

   (1) Matthew 4:1-4—"Then was Jesus was led up by the Spirit into the wilderness to be tested by the devil. And when he had fasted forty days and forty nights, he was afterward hungry. And when the tempter came to him, he said, If thou be the Son of God, command that these stones be made

73

bread. But he answered and said, It is written, Man shall not live by bread alone, but by every word that proceedeth out of the mouth of God." Our Lord was convinced of the reality of Satan. Throughout His ministry He countered the deeds of Satan.

(2) John 12:31—Jesus said, "Now is the judgment of this world; now shall the prince of this world [Satan] be cast out." The Lord was in conflict with Satan, and would soon triumph over him at the cross. Christ knew He was in conflict with a real adversary because He created him (Col. 1:16).

(3) John 14:30—Jesus said to His disciples, "Hereafter I will not talk much with you; for the prince of this world cometh."

(4) John 16:11—Jesus said, "The prince of this world is judged."

(5) John 8:44—Jesus said to the religious leaders, "Ye are of your father the devil."

b) By Paul

Ephesians 2:2 says all unbelievers are led by "the prince of the power of the air, the spirit that now worketh in the sons of disobedience."

c) By John

First John 3:8 says, "He that committeth sin is of the devil; for the devil sinneth from the beginning. For this purpose the Son of God was manifested, that he might destroy the works of the devil." To believe in Christ but not in the devil makes a mockery out of what Christ did and said. Understanding their conflict is basic to understanding the New Testament. First John 5:19 says, "The whole world lies in the power of the evil one" (NASB).

d) By James

James 4:7 says, "Resist the devil, and he will flee from you."

e) By Peter

First Peter 5:8 says, "Your adversary, the devil, like a roaring lion walketh about, seeking whom he may devour."

The New Testament writers clearly understood that God's purpose in sending Christ was to defeat the devil.

2. The activity of Satan

a) He tempted Eve (Gen. 3:1-6).

b) He tempted Christ (Matt. 4:1-11).

c) He perverts God's Word (Gen. 3:1; Matt. 4:6).

d) He opposes God's work (Zech. 3:1).

e) He hinders God's servants (1 Thess. 2:18).

f) He hinders the gospel (Matt. 13:19, 38-39; 2 Cor. 4:4).

g) He ensnares the wicked (1 Tim. 3:7; 2 Tim. 2:26).

h) He deceives the nations (1 Kings 22:6-7, 19-23; Rev. 16:14; 20:7-8).

i) He disguises himself as an angel of light (2 Cor. 11:3, 14).

j) He contended with the angel Michael (Jude 9).

k) He instigated the fall of the human race (Gen. 3:13-24).

l) He seeks to devour (1 Pet. 5:8).

m) He accuses God's people (Job 1:6-12; 2:1-6; Rev. 12:10).

n) He once had the power of death (Heb. 2:14).

o) The whole world lies in his power (1 John 5:19).

A Guarded Garden

According to Genesis 2:15, God told Adam he was placed "into the garden of Eden to till it and to keep it." The Hebrew word translated "keep" means "to guard." By implication, there existed a potential danger that required Adam to be on guard. In Genesis 3 the adversary revealed himself. So the very beginning of Scripture hints of the conflict to come.

C. The Experiential Evidence

The devil has manifested himself in many ways in our world today. Some are so obviously assured of his existence that they overtly and openly worship him. Also there are strange reports of healings and wonders associated with ungodly persons or activities that can only be attributed to satanic activity (cf. Ex. 7:11-12; 2 Tim. 3:8). They, too, give evidence of his existence.

II. SATAN—WHO IS HE?

A. He Is a Person

We have seen that Satan is a fallen angel. As an angel he possesses a personality. Angels also have proper names. They have all the properties of personhood: a mind, emotion, and will. When an angel praises God, it is an emotional expression. Unfallen angels will to defend God and fight demons.

1. His traits

   a) The ability to plan

   Animals don't make plans; people do. The New Testament often discusses Satan's attempts to deceive people and lead them astray. In 2 Corinthians 11:3 Paul says, "I fear, lest by any means, as the serpent beguiled Eve through his craftiness, so your minds should be corrupted from the simplicity that is in Christ."

   b) The ability to communicate

   Satan held a conversation with Jesus in the wilderness (Matt. 4:1-11) and with Eve in the Garden (Gen. 3:1-6).

   c) The ability to will something

   Satan has certain desires and wills to accomplish those objectives. For example, he took Jesus to the top of a mountain and offered Him all the kingdoms of the world if He would give in to his temptations (Matt. 4:8-9).

2. His accountability

   Satan is held personally accountable by God for his actions. Animals are not accountable—they have no biblical standard for moral behavior. But God has established biblical standards for man's behavior. That God said He would judge Satan (Gen. 3:15; Rom. 16:20) implies that Satan knowingly violated God's standards. Thus he is held personally accountable for his violations.

3. His names

   Satan is designated not only by personal pronouns such as you and he (Ezek. 28; 2 Cor. 11:14-15), but also by proper names and descriptive titles.

a) The anointed cherub (Ezek. 28:14)

That title designates Satan as one of the highest-ranking angels before his fall.

b) The prince of this world (John 16:11)

Satan rules an evil world system of angels and unbelieving people.

c) The prince of the power of the air (Eph. 2:2)

That means he has dominion in the atmospheric realm.

d) The god of this age (2 Cor. 4:4)

Satan is the god of this present world system. He propagates false religions, humanism, materialism, and preoccupation with sex.

e) Beelzebub, the chief of demons (Luke 11:15)

Beelzebub is a derogatory title meaning "Lord of the flies" that the Jewish people ascribed to a Philistine god. It came to be a synonym for *Satan*.

All those personal titles refer to Satan's rule, authority, and power. He is a person who establishes and directs a plan.

B. He Is a Spirit

1. His immaterial composition

Angels are spirits—they are immaterial beings. Angels are called "ministering spirits" (Heb. 1:14). Demons are called "evil spirits" (Luke 8:2) and "unclean spirits" (Luke 4:36).

2. His spatial limitation

Satan is not omnipresent like God. The book of Daniel gives evidence that when angels or demons are in one

78

location they must travel to get somewhere else (e.g., 9:21; 10:12-14, 20-21). When our Lord cast demons out of the demoniac near Gerasa, He sent them into a herd of swine (Luke 8:33). Demons and angels cannot be everywhere at the same time. Satan has the same limitations.

3. His visual manifestation

Satan has the capability to materialize in a human form. So do the angels. When two angels entered Sodom to rescue Lot, they were in the form of men (Gen. 19:1). They may have been uniquely handsome, for when the homosexual population saw them, they sought to sexually abuse them (v. 5). That's why God destroyed the city.

Before that, demons apparently materialized and cohabited with women, creating a demonic-human race (Gen. 6:1-7; Jude 6). Consequently, one reason for the Flood was to destroy that perverse race, thus eliminating the possibility of their impeding God's redemptive plan.

4. His immortal status

Angels are immortal—they never die. They live forever from the moment of their creation. Thus Satan is immortal. After death, humans will live forever as well, either with God or without Him.

C. He Is a Fallen Angel

The Bible records the existence of different ranks of angels. The highest-ranking angels God created are cherubim. They possess indescribable beauty and power beyond anything the human mind can conceive. It is their duty to protect God's holiness. They always appear surrounding God's presence (Ex. 25:18-22; Ezek. 1:4-28; Rev. 4:6-8). Sometimes they are seen proclaiming God's grace.

The Bible names three of the cherubim: Gabriel, whose specific task is to reveal and interpret God's purpose and program for His kingdom; Michael, who is seen as the general of the angelic army and the champion of Israel; and Lucifer, the most glorious creature God ever made. Lucifer

79

(Heb. *helēl*) means "son of the dawn," "shining one," and "star of the morning."

1. Satan's rise and fall (Ezekiel 28)

As a prophet of God, Ezekiel gave messages of judgment. One such judgment fell on the king of Tyre. He was evil, ruthless, and cruel. The pronouncement of judgment culminates in God's saying, "Wilt thou yet say before him that slayeth thee, I am a god? But thou shalt be a man, and not God, in the hand of him that slayeth thee. Thou shalt die the deaths of the uncircumcised by the hand of foreigners; for I have spoken it, saith the Lord God" (Ezek. 28:9-10). The king of Tyre was claiming to be God, and that's the grossest manifestation of pride.

However, beginning in verse 11, Ezekiel goes beyond the king of Tyre to the source of his evil, Satan himself. That is not an uncommon pattern in Scripture. Often the messianic psalms present David talking about himself, but underlying that is a reference to the Messiah. On one occasion our Lord said to Peter, "Get thee behind me, Satan" (Matt. 16:23). Jesus physically addressed Peter, but in reality He was talking to the source that inspired Peter's evil remark. The same is true in Ezekiel 28. God takes us behind the scene so we see who caused the king of Tyre to behave as he did.

a) His beauty

In verse 12 God says to Ezekiel, "Son of man, take up a lamentation upon the king of Tyre, and say unto him, Thus saith the Lord God: Thou sealest up the sum, full of wisdom, and perfect in beauty." This supernatural king was the sum of all God's creation. He was "full of wisdom, and perfect in beauty." If you wanted to know what God thinks is beautiful, you would have had to behold this particular angel in his original essence.

b) His preexistence

Verse 13 says, "Thou hast been in Eden, the garden of God." Obviously the king of Tyre had never been there, but Satan had (Gen. 3:1; Rev. 12:9). It is probable that this particular Eden is not an allusion to the Garden of Eden on earth, but to the paradise or Eden of heaven in the presence of God.

c) His talent

Then God described him: "Every precious stone was thy covering, the sardius, topaz, and the diamond, the beryl, the onyx, and the jasper, the sapphire, the emerald, and the carbuncle, and gold; the workmanship of thy timbrels and of thy flutes was prepared in thee in the day that thou wast created" (v. 13). In addition to being adorned by a plethora of glittering jewels, he is seen as the supreme musician in heaven. That gives you some idea of how God values music—He loves it!

d) His position

Verse 14 says, "Thou art the anointed cherub that covereth, and I have set thee so; thou wast upon the holy mountain of God; thou hast walked up and down in the midst of the stones of fire." Satan originally may have occupied a place of honor about the throne of God. "Stones of fire" perhaps refers to the blazing *Shekinah* of God.

e) His sin

But sadly, that glorious creature fell: "Thou wast perfect in thy ways from the day that thou wast created, till iniquity was found in thee. By the multitude of thy merchandise they have filled the midst of thee with violence, and thou hast sinned; therefore, I will cast thee as profane out of the mountain of God, and I will destroy thee, O covering cherub, from the midst of the stones of fire. . . . Thou hast defiled thy sanctuaries by the multitude of thine iniquities, by the iniquity of thy merchandise" (vv. 15-

16, 18). Satan propagated his sin and took one third of the angels with him (Rev. 12:4, 9).

God concluded, "Therefore will I bring forth a fire from the midst of thee; it shall devour thee, and I will bring thee to ashes upon the earth in the sight of all them that behold thee" (v. 18).

2. Satan's pride and punishment (Isaiah 14)

Isaiah 14:12 says, "How art thou fallen from heaven, O Lucifer, son of the morning!" You can almost sense God's sorrow over the great fall Lucifer suffered. How could such a thing have happened? The following verses make it clear that pride was Lucifer's downfall.

a) The expression of his pride

(1) "I will ascend into heaven" (v. 13a)—Since Lucifer, as the leading cherub, already had access to God, he was not simply saying, "I'll go visit God." There was only one place he could ascend —he was planning to take over God's throne.

(2) "I will exalt my throne above the stars of God" (v. 13b)—He was intending to usurp God's authority over the angels and take over as the ruler of heaven.

(3) "I will sit also upon the mount of the congregation [assembly]" (v. 13c)—According to Isaiah 2:2 and Psalm 48:1-2, the mount of the assembly is the center of God's kingdom rule. Satan was aiming to take the place of Messiah.

(4) "I will ascend above the heights of the clouds" (v. 14a)—Most commentators think that refers to the glory of God, not to the clouds in the sky. Satan wanted to ascend above the glory of God.

(5) "I will be like the Most High [Heb., *elyon*]" (v. 14b)—*Elyon* speaks of God's supremacy over all else. Satan wanted to be the Supreme One.

What unbelievable manifestations of egoism and pride! Jesus said, "I beheld Satan as lightning fall from heaven" (Luke 10:18). When he fell, he fell fast. His beauty was immediately corrupted. Every angelic being who followed him was doomed with him to hell forever—to a hell specifically created for the devil and his demons (Matt. 25:41).

b) The execution of his punishment

Isaiah 14:15-17 says, "Thou shalt be brought down to sheol, to the sides of the pit. They that see thee shall narrowly look upon thee, and consider thee, saying, Is this the man who made the earth to tremble, who did shake kingdoms, who made the world like a wilderness, and destroyed its cities, who opened not the house of his prisoners?" Satan is not only damned to the pit, but also is despised. His weakness will be obvious to all who behold him.

"He will be brought to the pit." This prophecy will be fulfilled according to Revelation 20:3. At the end of the Great Tribulation, Satan will be cast into the pit for the duration of the millennial kingdom. After being loosed for a short time, he ultimately will be cast into the lake of fire forever (Rev. 20:10).

Why Did God Allow Satan's Rebellion to Continue?

When Satan fell, mankind had not yet fallen. However, we don't know when his fall took place or if the world was yet created. God could have destroyed Satan and his demons immediately and ended the rebellion, or He could have suppressed the rebellion until another one occurred. But God chose to do something else.

He chose to give the rebels full opportunity to exploit every avenue of their power to its limits—from the time of Genesis 3:1 until the establishment of God's kingdom. Why did God decide to allow that? The Bible doesn't say, but I believe He had at least one good reason: to let the rebellion run its course as an illustration to all creation that nothing can ever dethrone God. When Satan's rebellion is finally put to rest, no one will ever wonder if God's authority can be usurped. Perhaps that is the basis of the magnificent heavenly praise we read about in Revelation 4:1–5:11. While the rebellion continues, our holy God shows His hatred of sin. But because He's a loving God, He redeems those who don't want to be a part of the rebellion.

Conclusion

A. The Reality of Spiritual Conflict

The conflict continues on every level in the universe. It's active at the throne of God because Satan has access to God (Job 1:6-12; Rev. 12:10). Demonic and angelic armies battle each other (Dan. 10:10-13; Rev. 12:7-9). Of course, there's also a war at the human level. Jesus said to the ungodly Pharisees, "Ye are of your father the devil" (John 8:44). The children of God and the children of Satan fight each other (2 Tim. 3:12-13). I wonder how many Christians realize that the entire universe is a battleground and that they are in the middle of it. Satan is contending for the souls of men and women, and so is God. We are to be on God's team, contending alongside of Him and equipped with His armor (Eph. 6:10-17).

Is there a devil? You better believe there is! Who is he? He is a person, a spirit, and a fallen angel. He's an active aggressor in a war against God and His purposes in the world.

B. The Response to Christ's Call

Every person in the world is either a child of God or a child of Satan. Jesus said, "He that is not with me is against me" (Matt. 12:30). If you want to align yourself with a fallen creature who is damned, that's your choice. Jesus said, "Ye will not come to me that ye might have life" (John 5:40). You can be on God's side only by coming to Christ.

If you are a Christian, I trust this study has given you new impetus to fight the battle, resist the devil, and refuse to let him have a foothold in your life or gain an advantage over you. God deserves all your praise and service. Satan's power over death was defeated at the cross (Heb. 2:14), but he continues to tempt us to sin. We must "be strong in the Lord, and in the power of his might" (Eph. 6:10).

Focusing on the Facts

1. What does Job 38:4-7 tell us about when the angels were created (see p. 70)?
2. Who created the different angelic powers (Col. 1:16; see pp. 70-71)?
3. Why were angels created (see p. 71)?
4. What is one of the most difficult theological questions (see p. 71)?
5. How many angels rebelled with Satan (Rev. 12:4; see p. 72)?
6. What is the philosophical evidence for the existence of a personal, active adversary against God (see p. 72)?
7. What did Jesus think about the devil (see pp. 73-74)?
8. According to 1 John 3:8, why was the Son of God manifested (see p. 74)?
9. List some of the activities of Satan as recorded in Scripture (see pp. 75-76).
10. What abilities of Satan are important evidences of his personality (see p. 77)?
11. Cite and explain some of Satan's names (see pp. 77-78).
12. Why can't Satan be everywhere at the same time (see pp. 78-79)?
13. What kind of angel was Lucifer? What was his duty (see pp. 79-80)?
14. Who was the source behind the evil of the king of Tyre (see p. 80)?
15. What phrases in Ezekiel 28:12-16 show that a supernatural ruler is in view and not a historical king (see pp. 80-82)?
16. Cite the details of Satan's fall (Ezek. 28:15-18; see pp. 81-82).
17. According to Isaiah 14:13-14, what did Satan want (see p. 82)?
18. What is the place of Satan's ultimate punishment (Rev. 20:10; see p. 83)?
19. What is God showing creation by allowing Satan's rebellion to continue (see pp. 83-84)?
20. Where was Satan's power over death defeated (Heb. 2:14; see pp. 84-85)?

Pondering the Principles

1. Since Lucifer, glorious as he once was, was susceptible to leading a rebellion against God, how much more are we frail humans capable of it! What can you learn from Satan's example to prevent yourself from rebelling against God? Satan's lust for power set him on a course for self-destruction. Read the following verses to discover how you can debilitate whatever temptations get out of control: Proverbs 2:10-11; 4:14-18; Luke 22:46; Romans 6:12-13; 13:14; 1 Corinthians 6:18; Galatians 5:16; 1 John 2:15-17.

2. James 4:6 says, "God resisteth the proud, but giveth grace to the humble." Many times we are guilty of pride. Read Luke 18:9-17, John 5:40, and Romans 1:21-22, 28-32. What makes pride so disastrous to an unbeliever? Read 1 Corinthians 1:10-12; 3:3-5. What does pride do to believers? What does Philippians 2:1-4 tell us should characterize our attitudes and actions? Because of pride have you been unable to forgive someone for his or her mistake, or admit that you made a mistake and are in need of someone's forgiveness? If such a problem remains unresolved, follow Christ's instruction in Matthew 5:23-24 and that of Paul in Ephesians 4:31-32.

5
Satan—Part 2

Outline

Review
I. Satan—Is He?
II. Satan—Who Is He?

Lesson
III. Satan—What Is He Like?
 A. The Titles
  1. Satan
  2. The devil
  3. The old serpent
  4. The great dragon
  5. A roaring lion
  6. The evil one
  7. The destroyer
  8. The tempter
  9. The accuser
 B. The Terms
  1. A murderer
   a) 2 Kings 11:1-3
   b) Matthew 2:13-18
  2. A liar
   a) His overt strategy
   b) His covert strategy
    (1) Saying that God is a cosmic killjoy
    (2) Saying that God is a liar
    (3) Saying that believers are inherently materialistic
    (4) Saying that God is a patronizer

   (5) Saying that trials cause believers to defect spiritually
   (6) Saying that God performs miracles for physical satisfaction
   (7) Saying that you can exploit God's promises
   (8) Saying that you can shortcut God's plan
 3. A sinner
 4. An oppressor
 5. A perverter
  a) The asceticism of legalism
  b) The abuse of liberty
   (1) Its condemnation
   (2) Its consequence
   (3) Its caution
    (*a*) Proverbs 23:1-2
    (*b*) Proverbs 23:20-21
 6. An imitator
  a) His servants
  b) His synonyms

Review

 I. SATAN—IS HE? (see pp. 72-76)

 II. SATAN—WHO IS HE? (see pp. 76-84)

Lesson

III. SATAN—WHAT IS HE LIKE?

Here we will define the character of Satan. A clear understanding of what's going on in the world depends on knowing what the adversary is doing. Paul warned the Corinthians not to be "ignorant of his devices" (2 Cor. 2:11). The better we are able to anticipate his activity, the better we will be able to defend ourselves.

What Satan Is Not Like

Satan is not like God.

1. He is not self-existent—Satan was created. That means he is clearly inferior to God.

2. He is not sovereign—Satan rules a domain of demons, but not beyond the bounds God established for him. Satan never rid himself of God's rule. His rebellion failed totally. Satan was exiled to the earth and the domain around it. He chafes against the chains of God's sovereign will, which allow him to operate only within his own sphere. The apostle Paul indicated that God uses Satan to accomplish His own ends: "There was given to me a thorn in the flesh, the messenger of Satan to buffet me" (2 Cor. 12:7). Paul asked God to remove it, but God chose not to (vv. 8-9). God allowed Satan to do something that would ultimately bring Him glory (vv. 9-10).

3. He is not omnipotent—Satan is powerful, but not all powerful. First John 4:4 says, "Greater is he that is in you [a reference to God the Holy Spirit] than he that is in the world."

4. He is not omniscient—Satan does not know everything. Many Christians wonder if Satan can read their thoughts. The Bible gives no indication that he can. Satan doesn't know everything because he is an angel, and angels don't know everything. That is evident in 1 Peter 1:12, where we find that "angels desire to look into" the mystery of salvation. There are some things angels don't understand. And if holy angels don't understand everything, there's no reason to believe a corrupted one would. While there is no indication that Satan can read our thoughts, he is good at predicting our behavior because of his knowledge of human nature. He has spent untold years observing our attitudes and actions.

5. He is not omnipresent—Angels may be fast, as Daniel 9:21 indicates, but they cannot be everywhere at the same time.

All angels, both good and evil, have limitations placed on them as created beings. That includes Satan.

A. The Titles

The titles give us information about what Satan is like.

1. Satan

He is called Satan fifty-two times in Scripture. Satan comes from a Hebrew word that means "adversary." He is primarily the adversary of God. But he is also the adversary of God's holy angels, as evidenced by his struggles against Michael and the heavenly angels (Jude 9; Rev. 12:7-9). And he is the adversary of God's people—of those who have identified themselves with the Lord Jesus Christ (1 Thess. 2:18).

2. The devil

This name is used thirty-seven times in the New Testament. It is derived from the Greek word *diabolos*, which means "one who slanders" or "one who trips up." He aims to maliciously slander God (Gen. 3:1), Christ (Luke 22:3-4), the Holy Spirit (Acts 5:3), the church (Rev. 12:10), the Bible and true doctrine (1 Tim. 4:1), and the character of Christians (1 Tim. 3:7). He attempts to defame anything that even is associated with God. Since he controls the evil world system (1 John 5:19), the world does not tend to have much regard for Christians.

3. The old serpent

In Genesis 3:1 we see him as a serpent, and Revelation 12:9 refers to him as "that old serpent." In 2 Corinthians 11:3 Paul expresses the following concern: "I fear, lest by any means, as the serpent beguiled Eve through his craftiness, so your minds should be corrupted from the simplicity that is in Christ." Characteristic of the serpent is his craftiness, subtlety, and deceit. In Ephesians 4:14 Paul warns "that we henceforth be no more children, tossed to and fro, and carried about with every wind of doctrine, by the sleight of men, and cunning craftiness, by which they lie in wait to deceive."

4. The great dragon

Revelation 12:3 says, "There appeared another wonder in heaven; and, behold, a great red dragon, having seven heads and ten horns, and seven crowns on his head." Verses 7 and 9 refer to him as the dragon. That name indicates the power and destructiveness of this beast. He is pictured in Revelation 12 as the terrifying general of the demonic army of hell.

5. A roaring lion

In reading about lions I have discovered that they tend to roar only when they already have their prey. They don't roar when they are stalking their prey; otherwise it would be warned of its enemy's approach. Lions are sneaky. Once the lion has cornered or killed its prey, it roars in triumph before devouring it. When Peter said, "The devil, like a roaring lion walketh about, seeking whom he may devour" (1 Pet. 5:8), he was warning us about Satan's desire to capture us and engulf us in sin.

6. The evil one

The Greek term *ponēros* is translated "the evil one" in John 17:15 (NASB). First John 5:18 says, "We know that whosoever is born of God sinneth not, but he that is begotten of God keepeth himself, and that wicked one toucheth [holds] him not." When God has hold of a life, Satan can't hold onto that same life. *Ponēros* refers to an intrinsic, internal evil. Satan is evil personified. And like all who are evil, he is not satisfied with his own evil, but wants to corrupt others (Rom. 1:32).

7. The destroyer

Revelation 9:11 says his "name in the Hebrew tongue is Abaddon, but in the Greek tongue hath his name Apollyon." They both refer to him as destroyer. Satan tries to destroy everything God has made. He attempts to destroy people through physical death (John 8:44) as well as through spiritual death (2 Cor. 4:4).

8. The tempter

Matthew 4 details Satan's temptation of Jesus in the wilderness. Verse 3 refers to him as "the tempter." Satan entices men and women to evil.

9. The accuser

Satan accuses believers day and night (Rev. 12:10), but Jesus is our advocate (1 John 2:1). Satan falsely claimed that Job had a conditional faith in God—that once he no longer had wealth he would curse God (Job. 1:9-11; 2:4-5). Satan is busy accusing us before God, perhaps saying things like, "So-and-so hasn't fulfilled what You required—he's not worthy of Your grace, love, and salvation." But Romans 8:33 tells us that no one can "lay any thing to the charge of God's elect." Jesus Christ has already declared us righteous, and God has declared us justified. As a result we have nothing to fear.

B. The Terms

The terms the Bible uses to describe Satan are more descriptive than his titles.

1. A murderer

Jesus shocked the hypocritical Pharisees, who falsely assumed they were the children of God, by saying, "Ye are of your father the devil, and the lusts of your father ye will do. He was a murderer from the beginning" (John 8:44). The first crime recorded after the Fall was Cain's murder of Abel.(Gen. 4:8). That's how Satan began his career as a murderer. First John 3:12 says that "Cain, who was of that wicked one . . . killed his brother." Murder is satanic. Satan entices people to commit murder. He himself tried to slaughter Israel many times so that he might thwart God's redemptive plan. If he could have destroyed Israel, he could have eliminated the Messiah, who was to be born out of that nation.

a) 2 Kings 11:1-3—In those days there lived an evil woman named Athaliah. Her son, king Ahaziah, had been killed. Verse 1 says, "When Athaliah, the mother of Ahaziah, saw that her son was dead, she arose and destroyed all the seed royal." She was Satan's emissary. As such she attempted to murder all those who had the right to reign. At that time in the history of Israel, the royal line of David rested with one person. If anything happened to him, the messianic hope would be gone. Verses 2-3 tell us what happened: "But Jehosheba, the daughter of King Joram, sister of Ahaziah, took Joash, the son of Ahaziah, and stole him from among the king's sons who were slain; and they hid him, even him and his nurse, in the bedchamber from Athaliah, so that he was not slain. And he was with her hidden in the house of the Lord six years. And Athaliah did reign over the land." God protected the one little baby that carried the thread of the messianic hope.

b) Matthew 2:13-18—Finally the Messiah came. So Satan set out to murder the newborn child: "When they [the wise men] were departed, behold, an angel of the Lord appeareth to Joseph in a dream, saying, Arise, and take the young child and his mother, and flee into Egypt, and be thou there until I bring thee word; for Herod will seek the young child to destroy him. When he arose, he took the young child and his mother by night, and departed into Egypt: and was there until the death of Herod, that it might be fulfilled which was spoken by the Lord through the prophet, saying, Out of Egypt have I called my son. Then Herod, when he saw that he was mocked of the wise men, was exceedingly angry, and sent forth, and slew all the children that were in Bethlehem, and in all its borders, from two years old and under, according to the time which he had diligently inquired of the wise men. Then was fulfilled that which was spoken by Jeremiah, the prophet, saying, In Ramah was there a voice heard, lamentation, and weeping, and great mourning, Rachel weeping for her children, and would not be comforted, because they are not." Through Herod, Satan tried to destroy the Messiah. But God protected Him.

2. A liar

John 8:44 says Satan "abode not in the truth, because there is no truth in him. When he speaketh a lie, he speaketh of his own; for he is a liar, and the father of it." You can never believe Satan because he lies all the time. Revelation 12:9 says he "deceiveth the whole world." Don't think you can enter into a dialogue with Satan that will reveal truth.

a) His overt strategy

Through the world's preoccupation with witchcraft and the occult, Satan has directed people's attention away from what's really important. Some people have a fascination with Ouija boards. Many people want to know more about the next world. I'm sure Satan would prefer that people be diverted into his overt activity and lose sight of his covert activity.

b) His covert strategy

Satan's covert activity is lying. Dave Breese said, "Witchcraft . . . is certainly dangerous, but it deceives only the simple-minded. Toying with Ouija boards or holding a reverence for fetishes can produce a dreadful spiritual infection. Their main appeal, however, will be to those limited intellects who feel more than they think. External phenomena may be interesting, even spectacular, but are limited in their appeal to reasonable people. . . . With witchcraft, orgies, seances and demon possession, he [Satan] has captured thousands. With false doctrine, he has subverted millions" (*His Infernal Majesty* [Chicago: Moody, 1974], pp. 15-16). The real work of Satan takes place in the arena of false doctrine. Ultimately he has greater influence when false teachers deny the Word of God than he does by instigating a seance. Satan's deadliest activity is perverting the truth.

First Timothy 4:1-2 says, "The Spirit speaketh expressly that, in the latter times, some shall depart from the faith, giving heed to seducing spirits, and doctrines of demons, speaking lies in hypocrisy."

"Seducing spirits" refers to Satan's overt work and "doctrines of demons" his covert work. You can see why we are commanded to study the Word of God: so that we might counteract Satan's lies.

Let's look at some of Satan's most influential lies.

(1) Saying that God is a cosmic killjoy

Genesis 3:1 says, "The serpent was more subtle than any beast of the field which the Lord God had made. And he said unto the woman, Yea, hath God said, Ye shall not eat of every tree of the garden?" Satan questioned God's concern for Eve by suggesting that God was nothing more than a tyrant who delights in making unfair laws.

(2) Saying that God is a liar

Eve replied to the serpent, "We may eat of the fruit of the trees of the garden; but of the fruit of the tree which is in the midst of the garden, God hath said, Ye shall not eat of it, neither shall ye touch it, lest ye die" (Gen. 3:2-3). However, God never said they couldn't touch it. Then the serpent said to the woman, "Ye shall not surely die" (v. 4). He was accusing God of being a liar.

Numbers 32:23 says, "Be sure your sin will find you out." But Satan says, "No it won't; go ahead and sin. Who will know?" Hebrews 12:10-11 says that if you sin, God will chastise you. The only protection we have against the wiles of the devil is the shield of faith (Eph. 6:16). You either believe God or you believe Satan. As soon as you believe Satan, your shield is down and you're vulnerable to his attacks. But as long as you believe God, you know enough to do the right thing.

(3) Saying that believers are inherently materialistic

Job 1:6-9 says, "There was a day when the sons of God came to present themselves before the Lord, and Satan came also among them. And the Lord said unto Satan, from where comest thou? Then Satan answered the Lord, and said, From going to and fro in the earth, and from walking up and down in it. And the Lord said unto Satan, Hast thou considered my servant, Job, that there is none like him in the earth, a perfect and an upright man, one who feareth God, and shunneth evil? Then Satan answered the Lord, and said, Doth Job fear God for nothing?" By that last question Satan implied that believers are inherently materialistic—that the only reason Job or anyone else would serve God would be to receive blessings. Many believe that lie about Christians. They accuse us of being devoted to God because we want our physical and psychological needs met.

(4) Saying that God is a patronizer

In Job 1:10-11 Satan continues his criticism of God's providence: "Hast not thou made an hedge about him, and about his house, and about all that he hath on every side? Thou hast blessed the work of his hands, and his substance is increased in the land. But put forth thine hand now, and touch all that he hath, and he will curse thee to thy face." Satan accused God of patronizing Job—of holding onto His followers by giving them things.

(5) Saying that trials cause believers to defect spiritually

God allowed Satan to take everything away from Job (vv. 13-19). But Job said, "Naked came I out of my mother's womb, and naked shall I return there. The Lord gave, and the Lord hath taken away; blessed be the name of the Lord. In all this Job sinned not, nor charged God with folly" (vv. 21-22).

But Satan approached God again (2:1-2). This time the Lord said, "Hast thou considered my servant, Job, that there is none like him in the earth, a perfect and an upright man, one that feareth God, and shunneth evil? And still he holdeth fast his integrity, although thou movedst me against him, to destroy him without cause. And Satan answered the Lord, and said, Skin for skin, yea, all that a man hath will he give for his life. But put forth thine hand and touch his bone and his flesh, and he will curse thee to thy face" (vv. 3-5). Although Satan had to acknowledge that Job trusted in God for more than his circumstances, he thought he could get Job to turn from God if his life was made miserable through physical trials.

Verses 6-10 tell us what happened: "The Lord said unto Satan, Behold, he is in thine hand; but save his life. So went Satan forth from the presence of the Lord, and smote Job with sore boils from the sole of his foot unto his crown. And he took a potsherd with which to scrape himself, and he sat down among the ashes. Then said his wife unto him, Dost thou still retain thine integrity? Curse God, and die. But he said unto her, Thou speakest as one of the foolish women speaketh. What? Shall we receive good at the hand of God, and shall we not receive evil? In all this did not Job sin with his lips." Satan's lie is that trouble will bring defection because only this life matters. But the opposite is true: often when Christians face terrible physical stress, they turn to God.

(6) Saying that God performs miracles for physical satisfaction

Matthew 4:3 says, "When the tempter came to [Jesus], he said, If thou be the Son of God, command that these stones be made bread." After forty days Jesus was hungry. Satan reminded Him that as the Son of God, He could satisfy His hunger by providing Himself with food. After all, God miraculously fed Israel in the wilderness, and they were only sinful people. But Jesus said,

"It is written, Man shall not live by bread alone, but by every word that proceedeth out of the mouth of God" (v. 4).

An Overlooked Miracle Worker

Today many people want miracles. They think of God as a cosmic genie—a supernatural magician who has a bagful of tricks. They claim that miracles are the evidence of their great faith. But a constant demand for miracles isn't evidence of faith; it's doubt looking for proof. People who constantly look for miracles or claim to perform miracles are probably in touch with a miracle worker who is often overlooked: Satan. He performs miracles all the time to satisfy physical desires and to deceive people into thinking that those miracles come from God.

My wife, Patricia, and I had an opportunity to meet with a couple who were new Christians. They said they had started getting together with some people who sought miracles. The wife went on to explain how her seven-year-old daughter would wake up in the middle of the night in a cold sweat claiming to have received wonderful revelations from God. They asked me for my reaction. I told them that not one of those revelations was from God. They were shocked. Then I told them that God already gave us His revelation—the Bible. Satan's big lie is that God isn't present unless miracles are continually being performed. Once people start looking for them, it's a simple task for Satan to perform minor miracles and captivate their minds, directing their focus away from the revelation of Scripture.

(7) Saying that you can exploit God's promises

Matthew 4:5-6 says, "The devil taketh [Jesus] up into the holy city, and setteth him on a pinnacle of the temple, and saith unto him, If thou be the Son of God, cast thyself down; for it is written, He shall give his angels charge concerning thee, and in their hands they shall bear thee up, lest at any time thou dash thy foot against a stone." Satan wanted Christ to exploit God's promise to take care of Him. Misrepresenting God's original intention, Satan would have us believe that God

will work on our behalf in spite of our unwilling-
ness to cooperate with Him (cf. Phil. 2:12-13).

(8) Saying that you can shortcut God's plan

Satan would have us believe that we can get what
we want our way—that we don't have to follow
God's plan. Having shown Christ all the kingdoms of the world, Satan said, "All these things
will I give thee, if thou wilt fall down and worship me" (Matt. 4:9). Satan suggested that Christ
bypass God's plan and accept his offer of all the
kingdoms of the world right away. By doing so,
He supposedly could have circumvented the
cross and avoided paying the price. But our Lord
was not fooled by that great lie. Neither should
we be.

3. A sinner

First John 3:8 says, "He that committeth [Gk., *poieō*] sin
is of the devil; for the devil sinneth from the beginning."
Satan is a habitual sinner. *Poieō* is in the present tense,
and here refers to habitual sin that has its source in the
devil. Satan is the basis of sin. Christ came into the
world not only to destroy sin but to destroy Satan as
well. John said, "The Son of God was manifested, that
he might destroy the works of the devil" (1 John 3:8).

4. An oppressor

Satan is the oppressor of the saints. First Peter 5:8 says
that he is "like a roaring lion walketh about, seeking
whom he may devour." Satan tracks down the saints
and tries to trap them in sin.

5. A perverter

Satan has taken hold of every good thing God has made
and perverted it. God made fruit for food and drink
(Gen. 1:29-30), but Satan can pervert it into alcoholism
(Eph. 5:18). God designed sex for us to enjoy within
marriage (Heb. 13:4), but Satan can pervert it into something lewd or adulterous (Gal. 5:19).

To see the effectiveness of Satan's perversions, let's examine one area where he has been particularly effective: food. You can't get drunk on food, but you certainly can be a glutton.

a) The asceticism of legalism

First Timothy 4:1 refers to Satan's doctrine of demons which was taught by men who departed from the faith. One of the things they taught was "to abstain from foods, which God hath created to be received with thanksgiving by them who believe and know the truth" (v. 3). Satan took the idea of a diet and perverted it so that in certain systems of religion, spirituality is based on diet. When the New Testament church was established, many Jewish Christians believed their spirituality was still based on their diet. Paul had to address that problem in 1 Corinthians 8 and in Romans 14-15. Satan would love for people to think that their spirituality is dependent upon what they eat. I'm sure some people think that spirituality is dependent upon being a vegetarian.

b) The abuse of liberty

First Timothy 4:4 says, "Every creature of God is good, and nothing is to be refused, if it is received with thanksgiving." Everything created by God is good, but this truth is not license to gluttony. But that's just what some people do—they refuse nothing and eat everything in sight. Realizing that abstinence is a false sign of spirituality, some overcompensate in the opposite direction and sin in the area of gluttony.

(1) Its condemnation

First Peter 4:3 says, "The time past of our life may suffice us to have wrought the will of the Gentiles, when we walked in lasciviousness, lusts, excess of wine, revelings, carousings [banqueting]." Gluttony is inherent in revelings and carousings.

(2) Its consequence

Deuteronomy 21:20 tells us that Israel stoned children who were so out of control that, among other things, they became gluttons. God is serious
about balance in people's lives. We are to be tem-
perate and moderate in this area.

(3) Its caution

(a) Proverbs 23:1-2—"When thou sittest to eat
with a ruler, consider diligently what is before
thee, and put a knife to thy throat, if thou be a
man given to appetite." What a great diet that
would be! Overeating is a serious problem in
our society, especially since so many people
labor behind desks without the balance of
physical activity.

(b) Proverbs 23:20-21—"Be not among winebib-
bers, among gluttonous eaters of flesh; for the
drunkard and the glutton shall come to pover-
ty, and drowsiness shall clothe a man with
rags." Those who eat or drink too much tend
to become lazy and avoid work. When you
don't make any money, it's difficult to clothe
yourself with anything but rags.

Gluttony is serious. God has given us the wonderful
creation of food to fuel our bodies, but Satan has perverted it to be a false sign of spirituality or a license to
overindulge. There is nothing that Satan can't pervert in
some way.

6. An imitator

The only original thought Satan ever had was to sin. In
his desire to be worshiped as God, he strives to be an
imitator of his Creator.

a) His servants

Second Corinthians 11:13-15 says, "Such are false
apostles, deceitful workers, transforming themselves

into the apostles of Christ. And no marvel; for Satan himself is transformed into an angel of light. Therefore it is no great thing if his ministers also be transformed as ministers of righteousness." Drunkards and criminals are not the kind of people Satan can use on a long-term basis. He wants respected religious leaders who teach false doctrine under the guise of true religion.

b) His synonyms

The Hebrew word *nachash*, translated "serpent" in Genesis 3:1, means "to hiss" or "to whisper." But it can also mean "to shine." Satan is the hissing, shining one. Even as a serpent, his beauty must have made quite an impression on Eve. *Nachash* and *Lucifer* are synonyms since Lucifer means "the shining one." Satan has always been an angel of light. He is a deceiver who masks himself as a messenger of God.

Focusing on the Facts

1. In what ways is Satan unlike God (see p. 89)?
2. Cite and explain each of the names and titles given to Satan. Explain each one (see pp. 90-92).
3. What does the devil attempt to do (see p. 91)?
4. Whose advocacy is greater than Satan's accusations (see p. 92)?
5. How did Satan seek to thwart the redemptive plan of God (see pp. 92-93)?
6. Although Satan isn't mentioned explicitly in the crime, why did he incite Herod to kill all the children in Bethlehem that were under two years of age (see p. 93)?
7. Why can't we believe anything we might hear from Satan and his demons (see p. 94)?
8. What does Satan's overt strategy of diversion accomplish (see p. 94)?
9. Explain the intent of Satan's covert strategy (see p. 94).
10. List the various lies of which Satan is guilty. Briefly explain each one (see pp. 95-97).
11. Of what did Satan accuse Job in Job 1:9 and 2:4-5 (see pp. 95-97)?

12. What has Satan done to the good things God has provided (see p. 99)?
13. In what two ways has Satan perverted God's provision of food (see p. 100)?
14. What do Satan and his servants disguise themselves as (2 Cor. 11:13-15; see pp. 101-102)?

Pondering the Principles

1. Satan attempts to slander God and believers by damaging their reputations. Evaluate your reputation. Look up the following verses, which stress how important our lifestyle is to the watching world: Proverbs 22:1; John 13:34-35; Romans 13:1-7; Colossians 4:5-6; 1 Peter 2:12-17. Ask God for His guidance on how you might improve in areas where you are weak. Seek to reflect God's truth in your life so that He may be glorified (Matt. 5:16).

2. Have you succumbed to Satan's temptation to doubt God's good intentions? If so, meditate on Psalm 34; 84; Romans 8:28, 31-32; and Ephesians 1:3-12. Have you believed Satan's lie that there are no consequences to disobedience? If so, meditate on Psalm 32; Romans 1:18–2:16, 6:15-23; and Hebrews 12:1-11.

3. Christ could have aborted God's plan of redemption by exercising His right to rule as King. Instead He paid for the sins of humanity (Col. 2:13-14) and became the suffering servant of Isaiah 53. Read Philippians 2:5-11 and Hebrews 2:5-18. What truths in those passages do you need to apply to follow the principle of humiliation before exaltation? Look to the life of Christ as a model of what you should be like.

6
Satan—Part 3

Outline

Review
I. Satan—Is He?
II. Satan—Who Is He?
III. Satan—What Is He Like?

Lesson
IV. Satan—How Does He Operate?
  A. In His Own Children
    1. By preventing conversion
      a) Hardened hearts
        (1) The types of hearts
          (*a*) The unresponsive heart
          (*b*) The impulsive heart
          (*c*) The preoccupied heart
          (*d*) The receptive heart
        (2) The result of indifference
      b) Blinded minds
    2. By perverting the truth
      a) Through false doctrine
        (1) A commentary on false doctrine
          (*a*) 1 Timothy 4:1-2
          (*b*) 2 Thessalonians 2:9
        (2) The core of false doctrine
          (*a*) Denial
            i) The authority of Scripture
            ii) The deity of Christ
            iii) Salvation by grace
            iv) The second coming of Christ

        (*b*) Deception
             i) Rebellion
           ii) Idolatry
    b) Through a damning lifestyle
    c) Through oppression
        (1) Lust
        (2) Physical illness
        (3) Mental illness
        (4) Death
  3. By persuading the nations
B. In the Children of God
  1. By creating doubt
  2. By instigating persecution
  3. By hindering ministry
    a) 1 Thessalonians 2:18
    b) 2 Corinthians 12:7
  4. By infiltrating the church
    a) Through false Christians
    b) Through false teachers
        (1) 1 Timothy 4:1-3
        (2) 1 John 4:1
        (3) 2 Peter 2:1-2
    c) Through division
        (1) The situation in Corinth
        (2) The application to today
  5. By tempting us to sin
    a) To trust in our own resources
        (1) David's census
        (2) God's condemnation
        (3) Paul's command
    b) To lose faith in God
        (1) Luke 22:31-32
        (2) 1 Peter 5:8-9
        (3) Ephesians 6:16
    c) To lie
    d) To lose sexual control
    e) To be preoccupied with the world
    f) To be proud
    g) To be discouraged

Conclusion

In 2 Corinthians 2:11 the apostle Paul says, "We are not ignorant of [Satan's] devices." We are expected to recognize his schemes, plans, and stratagems. Since we have the Word of God, which unmasks Satan's disguises and reveals his schemes, we have no reason to be ignorant.

I. SATAN—IS HE? (see pp. 72-76)

II. SATAN—WHO IS HE? (see pp. 76-84)

III. SATAN—WHAT IS HE LIKE? (see pp. 88-102)

Lesson

IV. SATAN—HOW DOES HE OPERATE?

Satan operates within two groups of people: his own children and the children of God.

A. In His Own Children

Anyone who doesn't know Jesus Christ is outside the family of God and is a child of Satan. First John 5:19 says, "The whole world lieth in wickedness [lit., "the wicked one"]." In John 8:44 Jesus says to unbelievers, "Ye are of your father the devil."

1. By preventing conversion

Satan is busy preventing people from coming to Christ.

a) Hardened hearts

In Luke 8:11 the Lord begins to explain a parable He gave in verses 5-10 about a sower sowing seed: "The parable is this: The seed is the word of God." The sower was spreading the truth of God's Word. Verse 12 says, "Those by the wayside are they that hear; then cometh the devil, and taketh away the word out of their hearts, lest they should believe and be saved."

Verse 5 tells us that the wayside "was trodden down." The path was rock hard. Therefore when the seed fell on it, it remained on the surface and birds ate it. When people with hard hearts hear God's Word, they don't receive it and the devil comes and takes it away. The devil is in the business of preventing people from entering God's kingdom, and he does so by snatching away God's Word.

(1) The types of hearts

   (a) The unresponsive heart

   Matthew 13:19 says, "When any one heareth the word of the kingdom, and understandeth it not, then cometh the wicked one, and catcheth away that which was sown in his heart. This is he which received seed by the wayside." The devil snatches away God's Word—it doesn't register in an unresponsive heart.

   (b) The impulsive heart

   Verses 20-21 refer to a person with an impulsive heart: "He that receiveth the seed in stony places, the same is he that heareth the word, and immediately with joy receiveth it; yet hath he not root in himself, but endureth for a while; for when tribulation or persecution ariseth because of the word, immediately he is offended." A person who makes an impulsive commitment to Christ has no real root or depth.

   (c) The preoccupied heart

   Verse 22 says, "He also that received seed among the thorns is he that heareth the word;

and the care of this age, and the deceitfulness of riches, choke the word, and he becometh unfruitful." That person is too preoccupied with the world to give himself to God's Word.

(*d*) The receptive heart

Matthew 13:23 tells us that "he that received seed in the good ground is he that heareth the word, and understandeth it, who also beareth fruit."

(2) The result of indifference

Jesus' parable teaches that the condition of a person's heart determines how he or she will respond to the gospel. The heart with which we are concerned here is the unresponsive heart. When the Word of God falls on a heart that is indifferent, callous, and unresponsive, the devil can come and snatch away the Word. Before the person can dwell on its significance, Satan removes its impact by bringing new allurements that are more appealing than the necessary commitment to God's Word.

b) Blinded minds

Second Corinthians 4:3-4 says, "If our gospel be hidden it is hidden to them that are lost, in whom the god of this age [Satan] hath blinded the minds of them who believe not." Satan blinds the minds of those who willfully disbelieve God. That is not to say that God wants you saved, Satan wants you lost, and you cast the deciding vote. Neither is it true that you'd like to vote for God, but you're blinded by Satan. It does mean that Satan can make a person blind to spiritual truth because that person has an unbelieving heart.

To people with hard hearts the gospel seems irrelevant. First Corinthians 1:18 rightly says, "The preaching of the cross is to them that perish foolishness."

2. By perverting the truth

Satan desires to pervert the truth so that what people hear isn't the truth.

a) Through false doctrine

J. Dwight Pentecost said, "Satan, of course, would rather not have to do this work of taking away the seed that has been sown. He would rather so control the one who is doing the preaching that something other than the good seed of the Word of God is proclaimed. Think of the work that Satan has to accomplish when the Word is preached: if there are 500 people present when the true Word of God is planted in 500 hearts, he has to have 500 demons to get into 500 different lives to take out that which has been sown. What an economy of operation it is if he can have those people who think they will be taught the Word of God hear some lie of the devil. He has had to work with only one individual instead of 500. But knowing that the Word of God will be proclaimed and that the truth of God will be declared, Satan has prepared to prevent the good seed of the Word from falling into the good ground so that it can bring forth fruit" (*Your Adversary the Devil* [Grand Rapids: Zondervan, 1969], p. 114). Satan would much rather pervert the truth than prevent people from receiving it. Even now he is actively perverting the truth by propagating false doctrine.

(1) A commentary on false doctrine

(*a*) 1 Timothy 4:1-2—"The Spirit speaketh expressly that, in the latter times, some shall depart from the faith, giving heed to seducing spirits, and doctrines of demons, speaking lies in hypocrisy, having their conscience seared with a hot iron." False teachers speak hypocritical lies, and it doesn't seem to bother them.

(*b*) 2 Thessalonians 2:9—Paul identified the Antichrist as "him whose coming is after the working of Satan with all power and signs and lying wonders." False preachers not only speak lies that sound like the truth, but also do deeds that appear to be godly.

(2) The core of false doctrine

(*a*) Denial

   i) The authority of Scripture

When Satan said to Eve, "Yea, hath God said?" (Gen. 3:1), he was casting aspersions on the truth of God. Satan will continue the same tactic until the end: "The time will come when they will not endure sound doctrine but, after their own lusts, shall they heap to themselves teachers, having itching ears; and they shall turn away their ears from the truth, and shall be turned unto fables" (2 Tim. 4:3-4).

   ii) The deity of Christ

False teachers invariably deny the deity of Christ (2 Pet. 2:1). And a denial of the deity of Christ destroys the doctrine of salvation. If Christ on the cross was not God Almighty in human flesh, then He didn't accomplish the atonement He purported to accomplish.

   iii) Salvation by grace

There are only two possible methods of salvation: divine accomplishment or human achievement. Paul argued in Galatians that a man or woman is not saved by human achievement, but by divine accomplishment. Satan argues the opposite.

iv) The second coming of Christ

Satan denies the second coming because it is connected with judgment. Most false teachers have a truncated eschatology because they can't face ultimate judgment. In 2 Peter 3:4 scoffers ask, "Where is the promise of his coming? For since the fathers fell asleep, all things continue as they were from the beginning of the creation." But Peter responded that not all things have continued as they were, and he used the Flood as a case in point (vv. 5-7).

(b) Deception

In place of the true doctrines they deny, false teachers propagate false doctrine.

i) Rebellion

Satan likes to suggest that rebellion against God is effective. But God wants the world to know that rebellion against Him will never work. That's why He is allowing Satan's rebellion to run its course. Satan says you can get away with rebellion; God says you can't.

ii) Idolatry

Psalm 96:5 tells us that "all the gods of the nations are idols." If man wants to worship a rock, I believe Satan often allows demons to impersonate the god that man thinks is in the rock. Psalm 106:36-37 says, "They served their idols, which were a snare to them. Yea, they sacrificed their sons and their daughters unto demons." While they were making sacrifices to idols, they actually were sacrificing to demons, who had impersonated their god.

Satan even promotes angel worship (Col. 2:18).

b) Through a damning lifestyle

Ephesians 2:1-3 says, "You hath he made alive, who were dead in trespasses and sins; in which in times past ye walked according to the course of this world, according to the prince of the power of the air, the spirit that now worketh in the sons of disobedience; among whom also we all had our manner of life in times past in the lusts of our flesh, fulfilling the desires of the flesh and of the mind, and were by nature the children of wrath, even as others." Satan wants to trap people in a damning lifestyle from which they cannot extricate themselves.

c) Through oppression

(1) Lust

Satan would like all men and women to abandon themselves to their lusts, and he has been successful in many cases. Romans 1 tells us that for the most part, the world did just that: "God . . . gave them up to uncleanness through the lusts of their own hearts, to dishonor their own bodies between themselves, who exchanged the truth of God for a lie, and worshiped and served the creature more than the Creator, who is blessed forever. Amen. For this cause God gave them up unto vile affections; for even their women did exchange the natural use for that which is against nature. . . . Even as they did not like to retain God in their knowledge, God gave them over to a reprobate mind" (vv. 24-26, 28). Notice that the body is the major feature of verse 24, the heart in verse 26, and the mind in verse 28. Satan perverts the entire person.

Verses 29-31 are a catalog of lust: "unrighteousness, fornication, wickedness, covetousness, maliciousness, full of envy, murder, strife, deceit, malignity; whisperers, backbiters, haters of God, insolent, proud, boasters, inventors of evil things, disobedient to parents; without understanding, covenant breakers, without natural affection, implacable, unmerciful." Verse 32 concludes that while those who have abandoned themselves to such things know "that they who commit such things are worthy of death, not only do the same but have pleasure in them that do them." Satan wants people not only to abandon themselves to their lusts, but also to encourage others to do so. We certainly see that in our world today. Many have lost control in their abandonment to the aforementioned lusts.

(2) Physical illness

The gospels tell of people who were oppressed by Satan's demons with a loss of speech (Mark 9:17-29). Others were made blind (Matt. 12:22), others had physical deformities (Luke 13:11-17), and still others had epilepsy (Luke 9:37-43). That is not to say all physical illnesses are caused by demons, but it would be just as extreme to say that none are.

(3) Mental illness

One of the great causes of mental illness is satanic activity. Mark 5:2 tells of a man with an unclean spirit who lived among the tombs in Gadara. Though the people often bound him (v. 4), he kept breaking his fetters and chains, constantly crying out and cutting himself with stones (v. 5). His insanity was the result of his being possessed by demonic hosts.

Mark 9:22 tells us that a demon so oppressed a young man that he was unable to withstand the demon's attempts to "cast him into the fire, and into the waters, to destroy him." I am sure that many cases of mental illness and suicide are a result of Satan's oppressing his own people.

(4) Death

In Revelation 9:13-18 John says, "The sixth angel sounded, and I heard a voice from the four horns of the golden altar which is before God, saying to the sixth angel who had the trumpet, Loose the four angels who are bound in the great river, Euphrates. And the four angels were loosed, who were prepared for an hour, and a day, and a month, and a year, to slay the third part of men. And the number of the army of the horsemen were two hundred thousand thousand [two hundred million]; and I heard the number of them. And thus I saw the horses in the vision, and them that sat on them, having breastplates of fire, and of jacinth, and brimstone; and the heads of the horses were like the heads of lions, and out of their mouths issued fire and smoke and brimstone. By these three was the third part of men killed, by the fire, and by the smoke, and by the brimstone, which issued out of their mouths." That demon-inspired army will destroy one-third of the earth's population. God sometimes gives Satan the power to take life.

3. By persuading the nations

Satan works among his own people by influencing governments and nations. When Satan was unmasked in Isaiah 14 and Ezekiel 28, on both occasions the prophets were speaking to a human ruler. Yet they were actually addressing Satan, who was influencing those rulers. Daniel 10:13, 20 refers to certain nations that were governed by men possessed by demons. Satan has always been active in politics.

When Satan tempted our Lord in Matthew 4:1-11, he offered Christ the kingdoms of the world if He would bow down to him (vv. 8-9). Although Satan is a usurper, as prince of this world he does indeed hold sway over the kingdoms of the world.

Ephesians 6:12 warns us that "we wrestle not against flesh and blood, but against principalities, against powers, against the rulers of the darkness of this world, against spiritual wickedness in high places." From the Tower of Babel until now, Satan has ruled the nations of the world with his demonic hosts. And while God has allowed that, He sovereignly restrains their activity through the Holy Spirit, the restrainer of evil (2 Thess. 2:7).

B. In the Children of God

1. By creating doubt

Satan loves to make Christians doubt—to make us struggle with reality. I have endured those kinds of struggles. Satan typically suggests to me that Christianity is a waste of time. But I know it isn't, and one of the ways I rebuild my confidence is by meditating on all the "I know" verses, such as Job 19:25 and 2 Timothy 1:12.

Satan tempted Eve to doubt God—to doubt His Word, His goodness, His concern, and His security. That's why Paul described the hope of salvation as a helmet (1 Thess. 5:8). When Satan attacks with his broadsword of doubt, it will glance off the helmet of salvation.

2. By instigating persecution

Satan loves to persecute the church. He's had plenty of practice with Israel. In Revelation 2:10 we see Satan persecuting the church at Smyrna: "Fear none of those things which thou shalt suffer. Behold, the devil shall cast some of you into prison, that ye may be tried, and ye shall have tribulation ten days; be thou faithful unto death, and I will give thee a crown of life." Expect persecution because Satan will instigate it.

3. By hindering ministry

a) 1 Thessalonians 2:18—"We would have come unto you, even I, Paul, once and again; but Satan hindered us." Expect Satan to hinder your ministry. You may develop a ministry and see it run smoothly for a while. But when you run into the first obstacle, don't immediately assume you're doing something against

God's will. Examine the obstacle first. It just might be Satan's hindering. The more effective your ministry is, the more he will try to hinder it.

b) 2 Corinthians 12:7—Paul referred to a hindrance he endured as "a thorn in the flesh, the messenger of Satan sent to buffet [him]." God allowed Satan to hinder Paul in that way to keep him humble (v. 9). Paul understood and was thankful, saying, "Most gladly, therefore, will I rather glory in my infirmities. . . . For when I am weak, then am I strong" (vv. 9-10). Despite Satan's efforts to hinder believers, he never short-circuits God's plan.

4. By infiltrating the church

a) Through false Christians

Satan leads unbelievers who appear to be Christians to the church, and it is very difficult for true believers to know if they are genuine Christians or not. Once accepted, they can create much havoc. Their life-styles don't match their claims, so they confuse the world about what a true Christian is. They often become difficult to deal with; and they usually try to get into positions of leadership, which gives Satan a voice in many decisions.

In Matthew 13:38-39 the Lord identifies these false Christians in the parable of the wheat and the tares: "The field is the world; the good seed are the children of the kingdom, but the tares are the children of the wicked one; the enemy that sowed them is the devil; the harvest is the end of the age; and the reapers are the angels." The only way the wheat and tares will ever be separated is by God at the end of the age (v. 40).

b) Through false teachers

Satan loves to infiltrate the church with unbelievers who become approved by the leadership of the church. Once established, those individuals disseminate Satan's lies.

(1) 1 Timothy 4:1-3—Paul promised that false teachers in the church would speak "lies in hypocrisy."

(2) 1 John 4:1—John warned the church that "many false prophets are gone out into the world."

(3) 2 Peter 2:1-2—Peter said, "There shall be false teachers among you, who secretly shall bring in destructive heresies, even denying the Lord that bought them, and bring upon themselves swift destruction. And many shall follow their pernicious [evil] ways, by reason of whom the way of truth shall be evil spoken of."

That's why God has armed the Christian with "the sword of the Spirit, which is the Word of God" (Eph. 6:17). Only by God's provision can we counteract the satanic infiltration of false doctrine.

c) Through division

Satan loves to divide the church.

(1) The situation in Corinth

Second Corinthians 2:5-11 shows how Paul was able to prevent further division in the Corinthian assembly. In verses 5-6 he says, "If any has caused sorrow, he has caused sorrow not to me, but in some degree—in order not to say too much—to all of you. Sufficient for such a one is this punishment which was inflicted by the majority" (NASB). Paul had previously instructed the Corinthians to discipline an immoral man in their assembly, perhaps the one mentioned in 1 Corinthians 5:1-5. Apparently he was satisfied that the man had been sufficiently disciplined.

Verse 7 expresses Paul's concern that the Corinthians cease being overzealous disciplinarians and instead be forgiving and gracious friends: "On the contrary ye ought rather to forgive him, and comfort him, lest perhaps such a one should be swallowed up with overmuch sorrow." Unnecessary discipline, rather than being remedial, can drive a person to despair. Once the person repents, he is then to be restored (Gal. 6:1). Paul continued, "I beseech you that ye would confirm your love toward him. For to this end did I write, that I might know the proof of you, whether ye be obedient in all things. To whom ye forgive anything, I forgive also; for if I forgave anything, to whom I forgave it, for your sakes forgave I it in the person of Christ" (vv. 8-10). Paul wanted unity in the church, and that meant the people needed to be willing to forgive. A lack of forgiveness only creates further division.

In verse 11 Paul says, "Lest Satan should get an advantage of us; for we are not ignorant of his devices." What are his devices? One is that he loves to split the church—and there's no greater way to do that than to deal with a discipline situation in an unforgiving and unloving way.

(2) The application to today

What is the general principle? An overemphasis on doctrine to the exclusion of love is deadly to any church. Satan is very subtle—he infiltrates a church that's doing something technically right, such as disciplining a sinning member, and tries to get them to carry it out in the wrong way. The church is built on two things: love and sound doctrine. Too much sound doctrine without enough love will bring about division. Too much love without enough sound doctrine will bring about confusion. Beware of either extreme.

5. By tempting us to sin

Satan tempts us to sin through our flesh (1 Cor. 7:5; James 1:14-15) and through the world (1 John 2:15-16). The following are some of the sins with which he tempts us.

a) To trust in our own resources

Satan wants us to trust in our own resources because we're no match for him when we're not leaning on God.

(1) David's census

As king of Israel, David desired victory in the many wars Israel was fighting. Consequently he wanted to ascertain the manpower of Israel. Satan took advantage of that situation "and enticed David to number Israel. And David said to Joab and to the rulers of the people, Go, number Israel from Beersheba even to Dan; and bring the number of them to me, that I may know it. And Joab answered, The Lord make his people an hundred times as many more as they are; but, my lord the king, are they not all my lord's servants? Why, then, doth my lord require this thing? Why will he be a cause of trespass to Israel? Nevertheless, the king's word prevailed against Joab. Wherefore, Joab departed, and went throughout all Israel, and came to Jerusalem. And Joab gave the sum of the number of the people unto David. And all they of Israel were a million and an hundred thousand men who drew sword; and Judah was four hundred threescore and ten thousand men who drew the sword" (1 Chron. 21:1-5). That was a mighty army!

(2) God's condemnation

God condemned David for his sin: "God was displeased with this thing; therefore, he smote Israel" (v. 7). Who enticed David to number the people? Satan. He wants you, too, to trust in your own resources.

(3) Paul's command

In Ephesians 6:10 Paul exhorts us to "be strong in the Lord, and in the power of his might."

b) To lose faith in God

(1) Luke 22:31-32—Satan tempts us to give up on God. That was what he wanted Peter to do: "The Lord said, Simon, Simon, behold Satan hath desired to have you, that he may sift you as wheat" (v. 31). Sifting refers to the process of letting the wind separate the chaff from the grain. But the Lord said, "I have prayed for thee, that thy faith fail not" (v. 32). I believe Satan was trying to separate Peter from his faith by blowing it away in the wind of adversity. You can be sure that since the Lord prayed that Peter's faith would not fail, it didn't fail. Satan would love to separate you from your faith in God, but our Lord prays for us as well (John 17:20-24; Heb. 7:25).

(2) 1 Peter 5:8-9—"Be sober, be vigilant, because your adversary, the devil, like a roaring lion walketh about, seeking whom he may devour; whom resist steadfast in the faith."

(3) Ephesians 6:16—"Above all, [take] the shield of faith, with which ye shall be able to quench all the fiery darts of the wicked."

c) To lie

In Acts 5:3 Peter confronted Ananias and Sapphira: "Ananias, why hath Satan filled thine heart to lie to the Holy Spirit?" When you lie or even shade the truth, Satan is at the source.

d) To lose sexual control

In 1 Corinthians 7:5 Paul says this about sexual abstinence in marriage: "Stop depriving one another, except by agreement for a time that you may devote yourselves to prayer, and come together again lest Satan tempt you because of your lack of self-control" (NASB). If marriage partners decide to abstain from their sexual relationship for any reason other than prayer, they are in danger of succumbing to sexual temptation.

e) To be preoccupied with the world

First John 2:15-16 says, "Love not the world, neither the things that are in the world. If any man love the world, the love of the Father is not in him. For all that is in the world, the lust of the flesh, and the lust of the eyes, and the pride of life, is not of the Father, but is of the world." When you are absorbed in Satan's system, you have effectively turned your back on God. That's exactly what Demas did: Paul said, "Demas hath forsaken me, having loved this present world" (2 Tim. 4:10). Such a decision reveals he was not a true believer to begin with.

f) To be proud

Paul cautioned Timothy that when choosing elders in the church, he shouldn't choose "a novice [a recent convert], lest being lifted up with pride he fall into the condemnation of the devil" (1 Tim. 3:6). The devil loves to exalt people, to make them proud; then they soon fall. When recent converts or immature believers are given too much responsibility, pride goes to their head and their fall is great.

g) To be discouraged

First Peter 5:6-10 says, "Humble yourselves, therefore, under the mighty hand of God, that he may exalt you in due time, casting all your care upon him, for he careth for you. Be sober, be vigilant, because your adversary, the devil, like a roaring lion walketh about, seeking whom he may devour; whom resist steadfast in the faith, knowing that the same afflictions are accomplished in your brethren that are in the world. But the God of all grace, who hath called us unto his eternal glory by Christ Jesus, after ye have suffered awhile, make you perfect, establish, strengthen, settle you." Satan will try to wear our faith down by bringing discouragement into our lives. But we need to cast all our cares on Christ, depending on Him (v. 7). Verse 10 assures us that when our suffering is over, God will have made us mature.

Conclusion

Satan attacks his own children by preventing conversion, perverting the truth, and persuading the nations. He attacks believers by tempting us to trust in our own resources, lose faith in God, lie, be immoral, love the world, be proud, and be discouraged. But we have a great promise: "Resist the devil, and he will flee from you" (James 4:7).

Focusing on the Facts

1. Who are the children of Satan (see p. 107)?
2. What does Satan try to prevent from happening to his children (see p. 107)?
3. What does the downtrodden wayside path illustrate (see p. 108)?
4. What type of heart does Satan prevent from dwelling on the gospel (see p. 109)?
5. What are the three ways in which Satan perverts the truth (see pp. 110-13)?
6. What will those who deny God's truth do as an alternative (2 Tim. 4:3-4; see p. 111)?
7. Why is a denial of the deity of Christ also a denial of the doctrine of salvation (see p. 111)?
8. What are the two possible methods of salvation (see p. 111)?
9. How are demons related to idolatry? Support your answer with Scripture (see p. 112).
10. In what kind of lifestyle does Satan want to trap people (see p. 113)?
11. In what ways does Satan oppress his people? Explain (see pp. 113-15).
12. What piece of armor protects the believer's mind from doubts (1 Thess. 5:8; see p. 116)?
13. Why shouldn't we be quick to give up when we are faced with opposition in a ministry (see pp. 116-17)?
14. How does Satan confuse the world about Christian truth and lifestyle (see p. 117)?
15. In what ways does Satan infiltrate the church? Explain (see pp. 117-18).

16. What was Paul concerned might happen to the Corinthian church due to their treatment of a repentant brother (2 Cor. 2:7; see pp. 118-19)?
17. On what two things is a healthy church built? What happens when the two are unbalanced (see p. 119)?
18. What was the nature of David's sin in numbering Israel (see p. 120)?
19. By "sifting" a believer, what does Satan hope to accomplish (see p. 121)?
20. Why shouldn't a new believer be put in a position of leadership (1 Tim. 3:6; see p. 122)?

Pondering the Principles

1. Have you ever viewed unbelievers as victims of Satan? They need to be reminded that by pursuing the course of this world, they are running toward a dead end. Although Satan has deceived people to the point of being content with a temporary earthly life, they need to consider the stark reality of both physical and spiritual death. Pray for an opportunity to share with a friend, neighbor, or relative that Christ became a man "that through death he might destroy him that had the power of death, that is, the devil, and deliver them who, through fear of death, were all their lifetime subject to bondage" (Heb. 2:14-15). Show them that they no longer need to be in bondage to a system in which they futilely search for meaning.

2. Untreated division becomes like a malignant cancer. Is your family or church suffering from the same problem as the Corinthian church (1 Cor. 1:10-13)? James tells us that pride and selfishness are the causes of many divisions (James 4:1-6). Read Philippians 2 to discover the keys to unity and to learn from the humble examples of Christ, Paul, Timothy, and Epaphroditus.

3. Satan tempts us to become preoccupied with his godless world system. According to the parable of the sower (Matt. 13:20-22), what causes an individual to be unproductive? Read the following passages and identify the instruction each one gives us to prevent us from being unproductive: Matthew 6:19-34, 19:16-26; 1 Timothy 6:6-12; and James 1:27, 4:1-17.

7
God's Invisible Army—Part 1

Outline

Introduction
A. The Reality of Angels
   1. The experience of John Paton
   2. The experience of Elisha
B. The Neglect of Angels
   1. Scholasticism
   2. Roman Catholicism
   3. Paganism
   4. Rationalism and empiricism
   5. Occultism

Lesson
I. The Existence of Angels
   A. Denied by the Sadducees
   B. Declared in Scripture
      1. In the Old Testament
      2. In the New Testament
II. The Origin of Angels
   A. The Work of Their Immortal Creator
      1. Colossians 1:16
      2. Nehemiah 9:6
      3. Psalm 148:2-5
   B. The Act of Their Independent Creation
      1. Before time
      2. By a direct act
   C. The Record of Their Innumerable Ranks
      1. Their number
         a) A multitude
         b) Twelve legions

Introduction

We live in an apparently infinite universe. The nineteenth century French astronomer Camille Flammarion said, "Of all the truths that astronomy has revealed, the most important to us, and the one in which we should take an interest at the very beginning, is what it reveals about the planet we inhabit, its shape, size, mass, position and motions. . . . Observation will show us that, far from being fixed at the centre of the Universe, the Earth is carried along by advancing time; propelled towards a destination which we do not know, it rolls rapidly through the immensities of space, carrying along with it the generations flourishing on its surface" (*The Flammarion Book of Astronomy* [N.Y.: Simon and Schuster, 1964], pp. 11-12). It's staggering to contemplate the vastness of space.

A. The Reality of Angels

People often ask me if I believe that beings exist in places other than earth. I do—the universe is full of beings. Then I'm asked if I believe in UFOs. I do, but not the kind people usually associate with the term UFO. The Bible tells us that countless beings fill the void around us. These amazing beings, who live in the heavenly realm, are known as angels. And since the creation of man, they have mingled in human affairs. Hebrews 13:2 even says "Some have entertained angels unawares."

1. The experience of John Paton

Billy Graham wrote, "The Reverend John G. Paton, a missionary in the New Hebrides Islands, tells a thrilling story involving the protective care of angels. Hostile natives surrounded his mission headquarters one night, intent on burning the Patons out and killing them. John Paton and his wife prayed all during that terror-filled night that God would deliver them. When daylight came they were amazed to see the attackers unaccountably leave. They thanked God for delivering them.

"A year later, the chief of the tribe was converted to Jesus Christ, and Mr. Paton, remembering what had happened, asked the chief what had kept him and his men from burning down the house and killing them. The chief replied in surprise, 'Who were all those men you had with you there?' The missionary answered, 'There were no men there; just my wife and I.' The chief argued that they had seen many men standing guard—hundreds of big men in shining garments with drawn swords in their hands. They seemed to circle the mission station so that the natives were afraid to attack" (*Angels: God's Secret Agents* [N.Y.: Doubleday, 1975], p. 3). Did God dispatch a legion of angels to protect His servants? It wouldn't have been the first time.

2. The experience of Elisha

Second Kings 6:15-17 relates an incident involving the prophet Elisha and his servant, who were both about to be captured by the Syrian army: "When the servant of the man of God was risen early, and gone forth, behold, an host compassed the city, both with horses and chariots. And his servant said unto him, Alas, my master! What shall we do? And he answered, Fear not; for they who are with us are more than they who are with them. And Elisha prayed, and said, Lord, I pray thee, open his eyes, that he may see. And the Lord opened the eyes of the young man, and he saw; and, behold, the mountain was full of horses and chariots of fire round about Elisha." That was an invisible angelic army.

The universe is occupied by angels. While they cannot normally be perceived by human vision, they do mingle in the earth. They exist in a dimension we can't comprehend. But just because we can't see them doesn't mean they aren't there. When the natural vision of the young man in 2 Kings 6:17 was enhanced, he saw the previously invisible army.

B. The Neglect of Angels

In spite of their reality, for the most part angels have been ignored. Perfection and righteousness aren't very interesting to many people—they are much more interested in learning about demons. That's largely because of the world's preoccupation with the occult. But did you know that there are almost three hundred references in Scripture to angels? That many references is too many to ignore. So why have holy angels basically been ignored? To answer that, I did some research in church history to find out what has led the church to minimize the study of holy angels.

1. Scholasticism

Scholasticism was a theological trend of the medieval church that combined biblical teaching with the opinions of early church fathers and respected Greek philosophers. Its adherents were often guilty of arguing over trivially insignificant and whimsical aspects of theology. Many of the arguments focused on angels and included such questions as: How many angels could stand at the same time on the point of a needle? Can angels be in two places at once? If not, how fast are they? Does a person get a guardian angel when he is baptized, when he is born, or when he is conceived? All that speculation embarrassed true biblical scholars, many of whom went to the other extreme of ignoring the subject altogether.

2. Roman Catholicism

The Roman Catholic Church made it a practice to venerate angels. In his book on Catholic theology, Ludwig Ott wrote, "From the relation of the good angels to God and to mankind there flows the justification of the angel-cult. That which the Council of Trent teaches as to the invocation and veneration of the Saints . . . may also be applied to the angels" (*Fundamentals of Catholic Dogma* [St. Louis: B. Herder, 1954], p. 119). The primary angel that Catholics venerate is Michael. In fact, the Roman calendar points to September 29 as the day to celebrate "Michaelmas." Two large and famous churches were built to glorify and honor Michael. One was built by Constantine just a few miles outside Istanbul, and the other one was built in Rome. Prior to the fourth century, angel worship was considered heresy. In Colossians 2:18 Paul warns us not to worship angels. In response to the worship of angels, the Protestant church downplayed any mention of angels.

3. Paganism

Nearly every system of religion has believed in angels at one time. The Chinese designed slanted roofs to prevent demons from gaining access. The Gnostics believed in aeons, demons, and demi-gods. Various religions believe in genies. Heathen philosophers referred to spiritual beings: Socrates referred to a good demon (daimon) that took care of him. With that kind of confusion in its midst, the church tended to withdraw from teaching about angels and concentrated on Christ.

4. Rationalism and empiricism

Once the world entered the period known as the Industrial Revolution, there was much more of an emphasis on science and technology. During the eighteenth and nineteenth centuries, man had become distrustful of revelation from God and looked within himself or to that which could be verified experimentally for answers in life. Therefore people began disbelieving in angels and demons. Only since we have moved from the ages of rationalism and empiricism into the age of existentialism (or experience) have we seen a return of interest in spirit beings—that primarily being an interest in demons.

5. Occultism

This movement has diverted many Christians from studying holy angels to a preoccupation with demons.

Little has been written on the subject of angels. That there are nearly three hundred references to angels in Scripture makes them well worth a serious study.

The Benefits of Studying About Angels

1. You will see God's tremendous sovereign control over the world and universe through His creative power, which includes the angelic host. When you see how they operate, you will gain a new perspective of what God is like.

2. God created angels to serve Him. An important part of their service to Him includes service to His children (Heb. 1:14). Studying how they minister to us is very encouraging.

In his book *Angels: God's Secret Agents*, Billy Graham reflects a good perspective to have when studying about angels: "I am convinced that these heavenly beings exist and that they provide unseen aid on our behalf. I do not believe in angels because someone has told me about a dramatic visitation from an angel, impressive as such rare testimonies may be. I do not believe in angels because UFOs are astonishingly angel-like in some of their reported appearances. I do not believe in angels because ESP experts are making the realm of the spirit world seem more and more plausible. I do not believe in angels because of the sudden worldwide emphasis on the reality of Satan and demons. I do not believe in angels because I have ever seen one—because I haven't. I believe in angels because the Bible says there are angels; and I believe the Bible to be the true Word of God" ([N.Y.: Doubleday, 1975], pp. 14-15).

Lesson

In our study we will examine three things about angels: who they are, what they are, and how we are to respond to them.

I. THE EXISTENCE OF ANGELS

A. Denied by the Sadducees

There have always been people who don't believe in angels. Some religious leaders in Israel didn't believe in angels: Acts 23:8 tells us, "The Sadducees say that there is no resurrection, neither angel, nor spirit." The Sadducees were the rationalists—the materialists—of their day. They were Jewish liberals who didn't accept the resurrection despite the teaching of the Old Testament on the subject. For example, Job said, "Though after my skin worms destroy this body, yet in my flesh shall I see God, whom I shall see for myself, and mine eyes shall behold, and not another; though my heart be consumed within me" (Job. 19:26-27). The psalmist said, "Thou wilt not . . . permit thine Holy One to see corruption" (Ps. 16:10). The Sadducees also denied the existence of angels, a display of their ignorance or disbelief of their own Scriptures.

B. Declared in Scripture

1. In the Old Testament

Throughout the Old Testament, angels are presented as personal beings who are the messengers and ministers of God. If all those references to angels were removed, we would be left with inexplicable events and gaping holes in the narrative. There would be too many problems without solutions. If angels didn't exist, we would have to accuse God of error since the Old Testament is full of references to His sending angels to do His bidding.

2. In the New Testament

Angels are an inextricable part of the New Testament as well. Who announced the birth of Christ (Luke 2:8-14)?

Who told the shepherds where to go (Luke 2:8-12)? Who came to Jesus at His temptation and ministered to Him after He had fasted for forty days (Matt. 4:11)? Who went to Christ's tomb and announced His resurrection (Matt. 28:2-7)? Who is coming to gather the elect from the four corners of the world (Matt. 24:31)? Who freed Peter and John from jail (Acts 5:19)? Angels. If those supernatural beings didn't exist, accounts of their marvelous interventions would be reduced to lies; spiritual warfare would be nonexistent; Christ's temptation would be meaningless; and the book of Revelation would be reduced to chapter headings since angels appear on virtually every page.

The greatest single testimony to the existence of angels comes from Jesus Christ Himself. He referred to angels on many occasions (e.g., Matt. 18:10; 22:30; 24:31; 26:53).

I believe in the existence of angels not only because of the biblical record, but also because I've encountered them. There have been specific incidents where I have known I was dealing with fallen angels. But I also know, though I haven't perceived them, that I have been assisted by holy angels.

II. THE ORIGIN OF ANGELS

A. The Work of Their Immortal Creator

Once there were no angels. That means they were created.

1. Colossians 1:16—"By him [Christ] were all things created, that are in heaven, and that are in earth, visible and invisible." The visible things created on earth include man, while the invisible things created in heaven are angels. They are given different names: "whether they be thrones, or dominions, or principalities, or powers—all things were created by him, and for him" (v. 16). Those names refer to the ranks of angels in God's well-organized invisible army—an army created by the Lord Jesus Christ.

132

2. Nehemiah 9:6—"Thou, even thou, art Lord alone; thou hast made heaven, the heaven of heavens, with all their host, the earth, and all things that are in it." God created heaven and earth, as well as the earthly and angelic creatures that dwell therein.

3. Psalm 148:2-5—"Praise ye him, all his angels; praise ye him, all his hosts. Praise ye him, sun and moon; praise him, all ye stars of light. Praise him, ye heaven of heavens, and ye waters that are above the heavens. Let them praise the name of the Lord; for he commanded, and they were created." Like the heavens and the earth, angels were created by the command of God.

It's clear from those passages that angels are created beings. God, "the King of kings, and Lord of lords . . . alone possesses immortality" (1 Tim. 6:15-16, NASB) in the sense that He doesn't have a beginning or an end.

B. The Act of Their Independent Creation

1. Before time

Apparently angels were created before time began—before the material universe was brought into existence. It's obvious that angels were created before man because some of them had fallen by the time Satan tempted Eve to sin.

Job 38:7 says that "the morning stars sang together, and all the sons of God shouted for joy." What are the angels (the morning stars) singing and shouting about? Just before this, God had said to Job, "Where wast thou when I laid the foundations of the earth? . . . Who hath laid the measures of it, if thou knowest? Or who hath stretched the line upon it? Whereupon are its foundations fastened? Or who laid its cornerstone, when the morning stars sang together, and all the sons of God shouted for joy?" (vv. 4-7). The angelic hosts were rejoicing at the creation of the earth, so we know their creation predates that.

2. By a direct act

There was no procreation among angels—they were all directly created by God at one time. They have no capacity to reproduce. That's what our Lord implies in Matthew 22:30: "In the resurrection they [people] neither marry, nor are given in marriage, but are like the angels of God in heaven."

With an instantaneous command, millions of creatures came into existence. Since they do not reproduce, there is no increase in their number. They do not die, so there's no decrease in their number. The only change came when Satan was banished from heaven with a third of the angels who followed him in his rebellion (Rev. 12:4). Apparently those angels became demons. But they will all live forever—some in hell, some in heaven.

We generally assume that all angels look the same, but I don't believe God created them to be identical to one another. I believe that like man, they were created in God's image. They were created with capacities we understand like intelligence, emotion, and will. I believe that God, by one command, called into being millions of distinct angelic beings.

C. The Record of Their Innumerable Ranks

1. Their number

How many angels are there? How many did God create? Let's look at some facts and some theories.

a) A multitude—At the birth of Christ there appeared "a multitude of heavenly host, praising God" (Luke 2:13). Not all the angels were present—just some of them.

b) Twelve legions—At His arrest, Jesus told the disciples He could have asked the Father for "more than twelve legions of angels" to defend Him (Matt. 26:53). Since at that time a legion consisted of three thousand to six thousand men, twelve legions would number between thirty-six and seventy-two thousand angels. That many angels could protect anyone against anything—after all, only one angel killed 185,000 Assyrians (2 Kings 19:35).

c) More than believers—Referring to how God loves His own and cares for them, Jesus said, "Take heed that ye despise not one of these little ones; for I say unto you that in heaven their angels do always behold the face of my Father, who is in heaven" (Matt. 18:10). The angels assigned to God's people report to God what happens to them. Those who believe that that verse teaches that every believer has a group of angels assigned to him or her reason that there would have to be at least as many angels as believers. That could mean there are billions of angels. However, that is just a theory, not a fact.

d) The same number as stars—Others claim there are as many angels as there are stars. How many stars are there? Astronomers have determined the positions of more than a million stars, but estimate that hundreds of millions remain unlisted.

Angels are often equated with stars because the terms are used interchangeably. In Luke 2:13 angels are called "the heavenly host," while in Deuteronomy 17:3 the "host of heaven" refers to stars and other luminous bodies.

e) Hundreds of millions—In Revelation 5:11 John says, "I beheld, and I heard the voice of many angels . . . and the number of them was ten thousand times ten thousand, and thousands of thousands." That's 100 million and untold thousands besides. Consequently I believe there are billions of angels in the universe.

f) An innumerable company—Hebrews 12:22 says, "Ye are come unto Mount Zion, and unto the city of the living God, the heavenly Jerusalem, and to an innumerable company of angels." There are too many to be counted.

2. Their organization

Millions of beautiful and mighty angels carry out God's commands. They sweep with great speed throughout heaven and earth. They are better organized than the armies of Caesar, Alexander, or Napoleon. They are organized into cherubim (Gen. 3:24), seraphim (Isa. 6:2-3), living creatures (Rev. 4:6-8), and thrones, dominions, principalities, and powers (Col. 1:16). They are led by the archangel Michael (Dan. 10:21; Jude 9), who is assisted by Gabriel (Dan. 8:16).

3. Their titles

Scripture refers to the heavenly host as the sons of the mighty (Ps. 89:6), sons of God (Job 1:6), angels (Heb. *elohim*, "gods"; Ps. 8:5, NASB*), holy ones (Ps. 89:5-7), stars (Job 38:7), and chief princes (Dan. 10:13).

4. Their location

Angels can be found in the third heaven, the abode of God (2 Cor. 12:2-4; Rev. 4:6-11). We can find them in the second heaven, which is the universe (Dan. 10:13). And they can be found in the first heaven—the earth and its atmosphere—interacting with people (Luke 2:13).

III. THE NATURE OF ANGELS

A. They Are Persons

Angels are not supernatural robots. They are persons because they possess attributes of personality: intellect, emotion, and will.

1. Intellect

   a) Ezekiel 28:12—Lucifer, in his original state, was "full of wisdom."

   b) Matthew 28:5—Following the resurrection of Jesus, "the angel answered and said unto the women, Fear

* *New American Standard Bible*

136

not; for I know that ye seek Jesus, who was crucified." Angels are knowledgeable beings who are able to communicate.

c) Revelation 17:1—Angels have an understanding of God's plan and are able to articulate it. John said, "There came one of the seven angels who had the seven bowls, and talked with me, saying unto me, Come here; I will show unto thee. . . ."

While they have knowledge of God's plan, angels don't know everything because they are not omniscient like God. First Peter 1:12 says the gospel is something that "the angels desire to look into." Although they don't understand everything, they are nonetheless intelligent.

2. Emotion

a) Joy

Job 38:7 says the angels sang together at the creation. Singing is a response to the emotion of joy. Luke 15:10 says, "There is joy in the presence of the angels of God over one sinner that repenteth."

b) Worship

Isaiah 6:2-3 says of the seraphim above God's throne, "Each one had six wings; with two he covered his face, and with two he covered his feet, and with two he did fly. And one cried unto another, and said, Holy, holy, holy." That's an expression of worship.

3. Will

Hebrews 1:6 shows God appealing to the angelic will: "When he bringeth in the first-begotten into the world, He saith, And let all the angels of God worship him." That God invited the angels to worship the Christ child indicates they had a choice to do so. Unfortunately, Lucifer's will manifested itself in a prideful way (Isa. 14:13-14), and that was the cause of his downfall.

Angels have personalities. They are not ethereal spirits floating around without personalities. And each one's personality is apparently distinct.

Only Temporarily Superior to Man

Hebrews 2:9 tells us that Jesus Christ, in becoming a man, "was made a little lower than the angels." Angels occupy a higher state than we do (Ps. 8:5)—at least for now. But someday we'll rule over angels. In 1 Corinthians 6:3 Paul says, "Know ye not that we shall judge angels?" In Christ we'll be exalted as joint heirs with Him, sharing in His inheritance (Rom. 8:17). In Revelation 3:21 Christ says we will sit with Him in His throne. But until then, we remain a little lower than the angels. They are supernatural; we are not.

B. They Are Spirits

As creatures, both angels and men are limited by time and space, are dependent on God for their existence and well-being, and are responsible to Him. Yet angels differ from us. The angelic realm is just as active and complex as the human realm. The difference is we can't see their realm, while they can see ours. They are spirits; we are not. Hebrews 1:14 says, "Are they not all ministering spirits?"

1. Their limitations

Angels are not made out of flesh and blood (Luke 24:39). Although they have spiritual bodies, they are still beset by certain limitations.

a) In space

Angels have spatial limitations even though they are spirits. They're not like God. He is omnipresent—His spirit cannot be contained in the created universe (2 Chron. 6:18). Angelic beings are confined to one place at a time, which means they have some kind of form, although it's one we cannot yet perceive. They must travel through space to go from one place to another (Dan. 9:21; 10:13, 20).

138

b) In time

Scripture often pictures angels with wings. I think that speaks more of their swift obedience to the will of God than of literal wings.

2. Their manifestation

First Corinthians 15:44 differentiates between a natural body and a spiritual body. Angels must have a spiritual body because they certainly don't have a natural one.

a) How angels appear to people

When God chooses to let angels appear before human beings, they always appear as men (the one possible exception being Zechariah 5:9). In every case the masculine pronoun is used to speak of them. For example, in Genesis 18-19 the two angels who visited Abraham and later went into Sodom appeared as men. They sat down with Abraham. They ate, walked, and talked with him.

Sometimes angels take on a dazzling appearance. Matthew 28:3 says of the angel who appeared at Christ's empty tomb, "His countenance was like lightning, and his raiment white as snow."

b) How people are affected by angels

Being in the presence of an angel can be a startling experience. Mary experienced mental turmoil when Gabriel greeted her (Luke 1:29). Panic and terror gripped Zacharias when an angel appeared to him (Luke 1:12). Great fear fell upon the shepherds when angelic messengers announced the birth of Christ (Luke 2:9). The Roman soldiers who were guarding Christ's tomb were so overcome by fear when they saw the angel roll back the stone that they fell over and became like dead men (Matt. 28:4).

Being visited by angels is a supernatural event—something a person could never forget.

Focusing on the Facts

1. What kind of function did angels perform in 2 Kings 6:15-17 (see pp. 127-28)?
2. Why has the church downplayed the existence and importance of angels during the course of its history (see pp. 128-30)?
3. How did the church view the worship of angels prior to the fourth century (see p. 129)?
4. Why was the existence of angels rejected during the ages of rationalism and empiricism (see pp. 129-30)?
5. What are the benefits of studying about angels (see p. 130)?
6. According to Billy Graham, what is the best reason for believing in angels (see p. 130)?
7. Who in Jesus' day denied the existence of angels (Acts 23:8; see p. 131)?
8. What is the greatest single testimony to the existence of angels (see p. 132)?
9. When did God create the angels (see p. 133)?
10. Based on Scripture, how many angels did God create (see pp. 134-35)?
11. What attributes do angels possess that qualify them as persons (see p. 136)?
12. What do angels desire a better understanding of (1 Pet. 1:12)? What does that tell us about the extent of their knowledge (see p. 137)?
13. What do angels have in common with man? How do they differ (see p. 138)?
14. When angels are manifested before people, what do they usually appear as (see p. 139)?
15. What effect have the appearances of angels had on people (see p. 139)?

Pondering the Principles

1. Balance and moderation are important in the Christian life. Too often we don't exhibit the wisdom and self-control of a Spirit-led life, and we overreact to circumstances, just as the church did in regard to the abuses in angelology. We must be careful to guard against overreacting to extreme circumstances so we don't forfeit the benefits of valuable truth because someone mis-

handled God's Word. We need to be like the Bereans, who "received the word with all readiness of mind, and searched the scriptures daily" (Acts 17:11). If you know someone who has overreacted to the truth or the abuse of it, prayerfully instruct him in the way of truth with gentleness and patience (2 Tim. 2:23-26).

2. God graciously sends angels to minister to His children (Heb. 1:14). It is easy for us to take for granted God's many provisions for our physical and spiritual welfare. Read Psalm 34 and 91. Thank God for His unbounded grace and faithfulness. Thank Him for His angelic host, which works on our behalf in carrying out His perfect will.

8
God's Invisible Army—Part 2

Outline

Introduction
A. The Deity of the Angel of the Lord
   1. Genesis 16:7-13
   2. Exodus 3:1-4, 6
   3. Judges 6:11-13
   4. Judges 13:21-22
B. The Distinction of the Angel of the Lord
   1. Zechariah 1:12-13
   2. Zechariah 3:1-2
C. The Identity of the Angel of the Lord
   1. His manifestation
   2. His ministry
      a) He revealed God's Word (Ex. 3:2-6)
      b) He called leaders into God's service (Ex. 3:6-10; Judg. 6:14-16; 13:1-5, 24-25)
      c) He delivered His people (Ex. 14:19-20; Judg. 6:14-16)
      d) He protected His people
      e) He interceded for Israel (Zech. 1:12)
      f) He defended believers against the attacks of Satan (Zech. 3:1-6)
      g) He confirmed the covenant with Abraham (Gen. 22:15-18)
      h) He comforted Hagar (Gen. 16:7-11)

Review
 I. The Existence of Angels
 II. The Origin of Angels
III. The Nature of Angels

Lesson
IV. The Ministry of Angels
  A. To God
    1. As ministers of worship
      a) Isaiah 6:3
      b) Revelation 4:6, 8-9
      c) Revelation 5:8-9, 11-12
    2. As ministers of service
      a) They offer priestly service
      b) They deliver divine messages
        (1) The birth of Christ
        (2) The law of Moses
          (a) Acts 7:38
          (b) Acts 7:53
          (c) Hebrews 2:2
      c) They assist God's rule on earth
        (1) By restraining wickedness
        (2) By controlling the elements
          (a) Revelation 7:2-3
          (b) Revelation 8:7-8, 10, 12
          (c) Revelation 16:3-4, 8, 10-12
        (3) By controlling the nations
  B. To Christ
    1. At His birth
      a) They predicted it
      b) They announced it
    2. During His life
      a) Matthew 2:19-20
      b) Matthew 4:6
      c) Matthew 4:11
      d) Luke 22:42-43
    3. After His resurrection
    4. At His second coming
      a) They predicted it
      b) They will participate in it
  C. To believers
    1. Watching
      a) They watched the apostles
      b) They marvel at the church
      c) They look for evidence of a wife's submission to her husband
      d) They watch the preacher
      e) They will witness the reward of believers

144

2. Revealing
3. Guiding
   a) To ministry
   b) To salvation
   c) To chastening
4. Providing

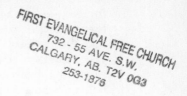

Introduction

The Old Testament speaks of one special angel who doesn't fit the mold of other angels. He is called "The Angel of the Lord" or "The Angel of Jehovah." His appearances are unique to the Old Testament. His first appearance is to Abraham, and His last appearance occurs in Zechariah.

A. The Deity of the Angel of the Lord

1. Genesis 16:7-13—"The angel of the Lord . . . said, Hagar, Sarai's maid, from where camest thou? And where wilt thou go? And she said, I flee from the face of my mistress, Sarai. And the angel of the Lord said unto her, Return to thy mistress, and submit thyself under her hands. And the angel of the Lord said unto her, I will multiply thy seed exceedingly, that it shall not be numbered for multitude. And the angel of the Lord said unto her, Behold, thou art with child, and shalt bear a son, and shalt call his name Ishmael; because the Lord hath heard thy affliction. And he will be a wild man; his hand will be against every man, and every man's hand against him; and he shall dwell in the presence of all his brethren. And she called the name of the Lord who spoke unto her, Thou God seest me." The Angel of the Lord is called God.

2. Exodus 3:1-4, 6—"Moses kept the flock of Jethro, his father-in-law, the priest of Midian; and he led the flock to the west side of the desert, and came to the mountain of God, even to Horeb. And the angel of the Lord appeared unto him in a flame of fire out of the midst of a bush; and he looked, and, behold, the bush burned with fire, and the bush was not consumed. And Moses

said, I will now turn aside and see this great sight, why the bush is not burnt. And when the Lord saw that he turned aside to see, God called unto him out of the midst of the bush" (vv. 1-4). Verse 2 tells us that the Angel of the Lord was in the bush; verse 4 tells us that God called to Moses out of the midst of the bush. Verse 6 tells us what the Angel of the Lord God said to Moses: "I am the God of thy father, the God of Abraham, the God of Isaac, and the God of Jacob. And Moses hid his face; for he was afraid to look upon God."

3. Judges 6:11-13—"There came an angel of the Lord, and sat under an oak which was in Ophrah, that pertained unto Joash the Abiezrite; and his son, Gideon, threshed wheat by the winepress, to hide it from the Midianites. And the angel of the Lord appeared unto him, and said unto him, The Lord is with thee, thou mighty man of valor. And Gideon said unto him, O my Lord." Here the Angel of the Lord is referred to as the Lord.

4. Judges 13:21-22—"The angel of the Lord did no more appear to Manoah and to his wife. Then Manoah knew that he was an angel of the Lord. And Manoah said unto his wife, We shall surely die, because we have seen God."

In four separate incidents the Angel of the Lord is equated with God.

B. The Distinction of the Angel of the Lord

1. Zechariah 1:12-13—"The angel of the Lord answered and said, O Lord of hosts. . . . And the Lord answered the angel." Here is a conversation between the Lord of hosts and the Angel of the Lord, whom we have already identified as God.

2. Zechariah 3:1-2—"He [the Lord] showed me Joshua, the high priest, standing before the angel of the Lord, and Satan standing at his right hand to resist him. And the Lord said unto Satan, The Lord rebuke thee." Here again another distinction is made between the Angel of the Lord and the Lord God.

C. The Identity of the Angel of the Lord

Who is the Angel of the Lord if He is God, yet distinct from God? I believe He is the Second Person of the Trinity—the Lord Jesus Christ Himself. The appearance of the Second Person of the Trinity in human form is known as a theophany, or more specifically, a Christophany (a preincarnation appearance of Christ).

1. His manifestation

The only member of the Trinity who ever manifests Himself is the Second Person. The Bible says that "God is spirit" (John 4:24, NASB) and that "no man hath seen God at any time" (John 1:18). The Holy Spirit, the Third Person of the Trinity, is of spiritual essence as well. He is never manifested visually. In the Old Testament the Second Person of the Trinity appears as the Angel of the Lord. But in the New Testament He appears as the man Christ Jesus, God in human flesh. *The* Angel of the Lord doesn't appear in the Bible after Zechariah because He became the incarnate Son in the New Testament (cf., Phil. 2:6-8).

2. His ministry

The ministry of the Angel of the Lord in the Old Testament parallels the ministry of Jesus Christ in the New Testament:

a) He revealed God's Word (Ex. 3:2-6; John 1:18).

b) He called leaders like Moses, Gideon, and Samson into God's service just as Christ called His disciples (Ex. 3:6-10; Judg. 6:14-16; 13:1-5, 24-25; Matt. 10:1-4).

c) He delivered His people through Moses, Gideon, and Samson just as Christ delivered His people through His work on the cross (Ex. 14:19-20; Judg. 6:14-16; Gal. 5:1).

d) He protected His people. Psalm 34:7 says, "The angel of the Lord encampeth round about those who fear him, and delivereth them." Christ protects us as well.

e) He interceded for Israel (Zech. 1:12). Similarly Christ is our intercessor (Heb. 7:25).

f) He defended believers against the attacks of Satan (Zech. 3:1-6), which is precisely what Christ does (1 John 2:1-2).

g) He confirmed the covenant with Abraham (Gen. 22:15-18), and Christ sealed the New Covenant with His blood (Matt. 26:28).

h) He comforted Hagar (Gen. 16:7-11), which is reminiscent of how Jesus comforts us (Matt. 11:28-30).

The Old Testament manifestation of Christ as the Angel of the Lord shows us that God has always existed as the Trinity. God hasn't assumed different roles in history; He has always been one, yet has existed as three distinct Persons.

Review

I. THE EXISTENCE OF ANGELS (see pp. 131-32)

II. THE ORIGIN OF ANGELS (see pp. 132-36)

III. THE NATURE OF ANGELS (see pp. 136-39)

Lesson

IV. THE MINISTRY OF ANGELS

   A. To God

      1. As ministers of worship

         a) Isaiah 6:3—The seraphim "cried unto another, and said, Holy, holy, holy, is the Lord of hosts."

148

b) Revelation 4:6, 8-9—"Before the throne there was a sea of glass like crystal; and in the midst of the throne, and round about the throne, were four living creatures full of eyes in front and behind. . . . They rest not day and night, saying, Holy, holy, holy, Lord God Almighty, who was, and is, and is to come. And those living creatures give glory and honor and thanks to him that is seated on the throne, who liveth forever and ever." The primary ministry of angels is to worship God.

c) Revelation 5:8-9, 11-12—"The four living creatures [cherubim] and four and twenty elders fell down before the Lamb, having every one of them harps, and golden bowls full of incense, which are the prayers of saints. And they sang a new song. . . . And I beheld, and I heard the voice of many angels round about the throne and the living creatures and the elders, and the number of them was ten thousand times ten thousand, and thousands of thousands, saying with a loud voice, Worthy is the Lamb."

Because of God's infinite worth and glory, and because of His excellence and beauty, the angels will praise Him forever. I imagine all the angels praise Him, but there seem to be some set aside who do nothing but praise God.

2. As ministers of service

a) They offer priestly service

Hebrews 1:7 says, "[God] maketh his angels spirits [winds], and his ministers a flame of fire." The Greek word translated "ministers" (*leitourgos*) gives us the English word *liturgy*. It refers to worship—to priestly service in the presence of God. That angels are like wind refers to their speed, and "a flame of fire" refers to their fervency and intensity.

b) They deliver divine messages

Psalm 103:20 says, "Bless the Lord, ye his angels, that excel in strength, that do his commandments,

149

hearkening unto the voice of his word." Angels are noted for their strength and obedience.

(1) The birth of Christ

According to Luke 1:19, it appears as though angels wait until God gives them specific orders to carry out: "The angel . . . said . . . I am Gabriel, who stands in the presence of God." Apparently Gabriel stood in God's presence until he received orders. His order in Luke 1:26-38 was to announce to the virgin Mary that she would soon bear the Son of God.

(2) The law of Moses

Galatians 3:19 says about the law, "It was added because of transgressions, till the seed should come to whom the promise was made; and it was ordained by angels." What part did angels have in establishing the law?

(a) Acts 7:38—"[Moses] was in the church [Gk., *ecclesia*, "a specially called-out group"] in the wilderness with the angel who spoke to him in Mount Sinai." We learn that angels were present on Mount Sinai, where Moses received the law.

(b) Acts 7:53—The prophets "received the law by the disposition of angels."

(c) Hebrews 2:2-3—"If the word spoken by angels was steadfast, and every transgression and disobedience received a just recompense of reward, how shall we escape, if we neglect so great salvation, which at the first began to be spoken by the Lord." The "word spoken by angels" refers to the law. The point the writer of Hebrews was making is that since no one could get away with disobeying the law spoken by angels, how could anyone think he could disobey the gospel spoken by Christ Himself?

150

Those references show us that angels were involved in the giving of the law. Apparently God authored the law (Ex. 31:18) and then delivered it to Moses through angels. After Moses broke the stone tablets in anger over the Israelites' sin, God rewrote the tablets (Ex. 34:1-5). It is possible that angels again delivered it.

c) They assist God's rule on earth

Angels assist God in plans He has for world governments.

(1) By restraining wickedness

We understand the Holy Spirit to be the restrainer of wickedness (2 Thess. 2:7), but angels also restrain people. Whereas the Holy Spirit's restraint is primarily internal, angels externally prevent people from doing evil. As an example consider Genesis 19:1: "There came two angels to Sodom at evening; and Lot sat in the gate of Sodom: and Lot seeing them rose up to meet them." Their arrival created much interest on the part of the homosexual men in the city. When the men came near to breaking down the door of Lot's house, where the angels were staying, the angels "put forth their hand, and pulled Lot into the house to them, and shut the door. And they smote the men that were at the door of the house with blindness, both small and great; so that they wearied themselves to find the door" (vv. 10-11). The angels restrained the evil of the Sodomites by blinding them.

(2) By controlling the elements

(*a*) Revelation 7:2-3—John said, "I saw another angel ascending from the east, having the seal of the living God; and he cried with a loud voice to the four angels, to whom it was given to hurt the earth and the sea, saying, Hurt not the earth, neither the sea, nor the trees, till we have sealed the servants of our God in their

151

foreheads." Those angels were preparing to bring God's plagues on the world by letting go of their control of the elements (v. 1).

(b) Revelation 8:7-8, 10, 12—Here the angels blow the trumpets of judgment: "The first angel sounded, there followed hail and fire mixed with blood. . . . The second angel sounded, and, as it were, a great mountain burning with fire was cast into the sea. . . . The third angel sounded, and there fell a great star from heaven, burning as though it were a lamp, and it fell upon the third part of the rivers, and upon the fountains of waters. . . . The fourth angel sounded, and the third part of the sun was smitten, and the third part of the moon, and the third part of the stars." Terrible catastrophes will occur in judgment as a result of the angels' power over the elements.

(c) Revelation 16:3-4, 8, 10-12—Here is a sampling of the bowl judgments: "The second angel poured out his bowl upon the sea, and it became like the blood of a dead man; and every living soul died in the sea. And the third angel poured out his bowl upon the rivers and fountains of waters, and they became blood. . . . The fourth angel poured out his bowl upon the sun, and power was given unto him to scorch men with fire. . . . The fifth angel poured out his bowl upon the throne of the beast, and his kingdom was full of darkness; and they gnawed their tongues for pain, and blasphemed the God of heaven because of their pains and their sores, and repented not of their deeds. And the sixth angel poured out his bowl upon the great river, Euphrates, and its water was dried up."

Angels have God-given power over the elements. The Lord will use them to bring about the most terrible catastrophes in the Great Tribulation.

(3) By controlling the nations

Angels are active behind the scene of governments. Demons fight to control nations and societies. The holy angels counteract their control.
Daniel said, "I saw in the visions of my head
upon my bed, and, behold, a watcher and an
holy one [an angel] came down from heaven. . . .
This matter is by the decree of the watchers, and
the demand by the word of the holy ones, to the
intent that the living may know that the Most
High ruleth in the kingdom of men, and giveth it
to whomsoever he will, and setteth up over it the
basest of men" (4:13, 17). Even the worst officials
in government are there because God has allowed
it. But angels watch over them all and carry out
God's plan.

B. To Christ

How did angels minister to Jesus Christ, and how will they
serve Him in the future?

1. At His birth

a) They predicted it

Luke 1:26-31 tells us about the prediction: "The angel, Gabriel, was sent from God unto a city of Galilee,
named Nazareth, to a virgin espoused to a man
whose name was Joseph, of the house of David; and
the virgin's name was Mary. And the angel came in
unto her, and said, Hail, thou who art highly fa-
vored, the Lord is with thee; blessed art thou among
women. And when she saw him, she was troubled at
his saying, and considered in her mind what manner
of greeting this should be. And the angel said unto
her, Fear not, Mary; for thou hast found favor with
God. And, behold, thou shalt conceive in thy womb,
and bring forth a son, and shalt call his name Jesus."
Angels were the first to tell Mary and Joseph that the
Messiah would be born to them (Matt. 1:20-21).

b) They announced it

> Luke 2:8-14 says, "There were . . . shepherds abiding in the field, keeping watch over their flock by night. And, lo, an angel of the Lord came upon them, and the glory of the Lord shown round about them; and they were very much afraid. And the angel said unto them, Fear not; for, behold, I bring you good tidings of great joy, which shall be to all people. For unto you is born this day in the city of David a Savior, who is Christ the Lord. . . . And suddenly there was with the angel a multitude of the heavenly host, praising God, and saying, Glory to God in the highest, and on earth peace, good will toward men."

2. During His life

A study of the life of Christ reveals that angels provided Him with protection and care. A beautiful expression of God's love is seen in the tender care He showed toward Christ in dispatching angels to minister to Him. That ought to give us great confidence, for God also dispatches angels to care for us.

a) Matthew 2:19-20—"When Herod was dead, behold, an angel of the Lord appeareth in a dream to Joseph in Egypt, saying, Arise, and take the young child and his mother, and go into the land of Israel; for they are dead who sought the young child's life." Previously an angel had appeared to Joseph and told him to go to Egypt to escape Herod, who planned to kill the child (v. 13). An angel warned them to leave Israel, and an angel told them to return.

b) Matthew 4:6—"It is written, He shall give his angels charge concerning thee, and in their hands they shall bear thee up, lest at any time thou dash thy foot against a stone." The devil quoted that Old Testament promise from Psalm 91 in the hopes of getting Jesus to abuse God's protection by jumping off the roof of the Temple. The devil was right—God's angels do protect Jesus. Be warned: the devil knows Scripture, and he will use it to his advantage to disarm the undiscerning.

c) Matthew 4:11—After Jesus had been tempted following His forty-day fast, "the devil leaveth him, and, behold, angels came and ministered to him." What did the angels do for Him? They probably brought Him food and did whatever they needed to comfort Him and meet His needs.

d) Luke 22:42-43—Jesus agonized in the Garden of Gethsemane, praying, "Father, if thou be willing, remove this cup from me, nevertheless, not my will, but thine, be done. And there appeared an angel unto him from heaven, strengthening him."

3. After His resurrection

Notice that we just went from Christ's earthly life to the resurrection. Angels were absent while Christ was crucified—a time when He could have used their help the most. But He purposely didn't (Matt. 26:53). If Jesus had circumvented God's redemptive plan by calling twelve legions of angels to rescue Him, we wouldn't be here as members of Christ's church. We'd be destined for eternal hell (1 Cor. 15:17).

In Matthew 28:1-6 we see angels announce the resurrection of Christ: "In the end of the sabbath, as it began to dawn toward the first day of the week, came Mary Magdalene and the other Mary to see the sepulcher. And, behold, there was a great earthquake; for an angel of the Lord descended from heaven, and came and rolled back the stone from the door, and sat upon it. His countenance was like lightning, and his raiment white as snow; and for fear of him the keepers did shake, and became as dead men. And the angel answered and said unto the women, Fear not; for I know that ye seek Jesus, who was crucified. He is not here; for he is risen, as he said. Come, see the place where the Lord lay" (cf. Luke 24:4-7).

4. At His second coming

a) They predicted it

As Jesus ascended into heaven and the disciples gazed up at Him, "two men stood by them in white

155

apparel; who also said, Ye men of Galilee, why stand ye gazing up into heaven? This same Jesus, who is taken up from you into heaven, shall so come in like manner as ye have seen him go into heaven" (Acts 1:10-11). The angels predicted the second coming of Christ.

b) They will participate in it

Matthew 25:31 says, "When the Son of man shall come in his glory . . . all the holy angels [will come] with him."

C. To believers

Angels minister to believers in many ways. Hebrews 1:14 says they are "ministering spirits, sent forth to minister for them who shall be heirs of salvation." We are the heirs of salvation, and God sends His angels to minister to us.

Did you know that angels love you? An angel addressed Daniel, saying, "O Daniel, a man greatly beloved" (Dan. 10:11). The angel loved Daniel because God loved Daniel. Since angels love what God loves, angels love us because God loves us. That means they are not unwilling in their service to us; they minister to us out of love. They love us so much that they rejoice when we come to Christ (Luke 15:10). We have the Holy Spirit dwelling in us, ministering to our spiritual needs; and we have angels around us taking care of our physical needs.

1. Watching

Angels keep watch over us. I doubt we are ever out of sight of the watchful eye of angels.

a) They watched the apostles—In 1 Corinthians 4:9 Paul says, "I think that God hath set forth us, the apostles, last . . . for we are made a spectacle unto the world, and to angels, and to men."

b) They marvel at the church—Ephesians 3:10 says, "Now, unto the principalities and powers in heavenly places, might be known by the church the manifold wisdom of God." The angels watch us to see God's wisdom on display. As a result of seeing how wise He is, they worship and praise His name.

c) They look for evidence of a wife's submission to her husband—In 1 Corinthians 11:3, 10 Paul says, "I would have you know the head of every man is Christ; and the head of the woman is the man; and the head of Christ is God. . . . For this cause ought the woman to have authority on her head because of the angels." This passage conveys the idea that wives are to submit to their husbands' authority. Angels watch to see that wives are submissive.

d) They watch the preacher—In the context of pastoral instruction, Paul exhorted Timothy not to ordain anyone too soon, to take a little wine for medicinal purposes, to see that elders rule well, to make sure the elders are fairly compensated, and not to accuse an elder (1 Tim. 5:17-20, 22-25). In the midst of that discussion Paul said, "I charge thee before God, and the Lord Jesus Christ, *and the elect angels*, that thou observe these things without preferring one before another, doing nothing by partiality" (v. 21, emphasis added).

e) They will witness the reward of believers—Matthew 16:27 says, "The Son of man shall come in the glory of his Father with his angels, and then he shall reward every man according to his works."

2. Revealing

Angels reveal truth. Much of Daniel and Revelation were delivered through the revelatory work of angels (Dan. 9:20–12:13; Rev. 1:1). God was the author, the Holy Spirit provided the inspiration, and angels were the agents who delivered it. Let me add this: if someone suggests they have received a revelation from God or an angel, don't believe him. The angels are no longer delivering God's Word (Heb. 1:1; 2:2-3).

3. Guiding

The Holy Spirit takes an internal role in guiding the believer, but the angels take an external role.

a) To ministry

As Philip preached to large crowds in Samaria, he performed miracles to support the authority of his message (Acts 8:5-6). During the course of his ministry, "an angel of the Lord spoke unto Philip, saying, Arise, and go toward the south unto the way that goeth down from Jerusalem unto Gaza, which is desert. He arose and went; and, behold, a man of Ethiopia, an eunuch of great authority" (vv. 26-27). Philip had a wonderful conversation with him and led him to Christ (vv. 29-39). An angel guided Philip out of one ministry into a different one for the Lord.

b) To salvation

In Caesarea a devout man named Cornelius saw "an angel of God coming in to him, and saying unto him, Cornelius. And when he looked on him, he was afraid, and said, What is it, Lord? And he said unto him, Thy prayers and thine alms are come up for a memorial before God. And now send men to Joppa, and call for one Simon, whose surname is Peter" (Acts 10:3-5). Later we see Peter's account of the same incident: "He [Cornelius] showed us how he had seen an angel in his house, who stood and said unto him, Send men to Joppa, and call for Simon, whose surname is Peter, who shall tell thee words, by which thou and all thy house shall be saved" (Acts 11:13-14).

c) To chastening

Included in the guiding ministry of angels is chastening. As the Lord guides us, He may have to discipline us to keep us in line. Let's look at how chastening was necessary for David in the following incident: "Satan stood up against Israel, and enticed David to number Israel" (1 Chron. 21:1). David's sin was in depending on the number of people he had in his army instead of on God.

The narrative continues: "David's heart smote him after he had numbered the people. And David said unto the Lord, I have sinned greatly in what I have done; and now, I beseech thee, O Lord, take away the iniquity of thy servant; for I have done very foolishly. . . . So [the prophet] Gad came to David and told him, and said unto him, Shall seven years of famine come unto thee in thy land? Or wilt thou flee three months before thine enemies, while they pursue thee? Or wilt thou that there be three days' pestilence in thy land? Now consider, and see what answer I shall return to him who sent me. And David said unto Gad, I am in deep distress; let us fall, now, into the hand of the Lord; for his mercies are great. And let me not fall into the hand of man. So the Lord sent a pestilence upon Israel from the morning even to the time appointed; and there died of the people, from Dan even to Beer-sheba, seventy thousand men. And when the angel stretched out his hand upon Jerusalem to destroy it, the Lord repented of the evil, and said to the angel who destroyed the people, It is enough; stay now thine hand" (2 Sam. 24:10, 13-16). God had to send an angel to take life in chastening His servant David.

4. Providing

When Elijah heard that the evil queen Jezebel was after him for destroying the priests of Baal, he panicked and ran out of town (1 Kings 19:1-3). Verse 4 picks up the story: "He himself went a day's journey into the wilderness, and came and sat down under a juniper tree. And he requested for himself that he might die, and said, It is enough! Now, O Lord, take away my life; for I am not better than my fathers. And as he lay and slept under a juniper tree, behold, an angel touched him, and said unto him, Arise, and eat. And he looked, and, behold, there was a cake baked on the coals, and a cruse of water at his head. And he did eat and drink, and lay down again. And the angel of the Lord came again the second time, and touched him, and said, Arise and eat, because

159

the journey is too great for thee. And he arose, and did eat and drink, and went in the strength of that food forty days and forty nights unto Horeb, the mount of God" (vv. 4-8). An angel provided support for the physically and emotionally exhausted prophet.

Angels watch us. In the past they revealed God's truth. In the present they guide us, even if they must lead us into chastisement. God also sends them to meet our needs.

Focusing on the Facts

1. With whom is the Angel of the Lord identified in the Old Testament (see pp. 145-46)?
2. How is the Angel of the Lord distinguished from God in Zechariah (see p. 146)?
3. What is a Christophany? How does that apply to the Angel of the Lord (see p. 147)?
4. How do the ministries of the Angel of the Lord and Christ parallel each other (see pp. 147-48)?
5. How do angels minister to God (see pp. 148-49)?
6. What message did Gabriel deliver in Luke 1:26-38 (see p. 150)?
7. What does the book of Revelation tell us about angels' control over the elements (see pp. 151-52)?
8. In what way are angels and demons active in the unfolding plan of history (see p. 153)?
9. What two things did angels do in regard to Christ's birth (see pp. 153-54)?
10. How did the angels protect Jesus as a child (Matt. 2:19-20; see p. 154)?
11. What is significant about the absence of angels at the crucifixion (see p. 155)?
12. What displays the wisdom of God to angels (Eph. 3:10; see pp. 156-57)?
13. What do angels look for in Christian wives? in pastors (see p. 157)?
14. In what ways do angels guide us (see pp. 158-59)?
15. What did an angel provide for Elijah (1 Kings 19:4-8; see pp. 159-60)?

Pondering the Principles

1. Do your own in-depth study on angels by examining Hebrews 1-2. Divide a piece of paper in half and list the qualities attributed to the Son of God on one side and the corresponding qualities of angels on the other. As you analyze chapter 1, consider Christ's relationship to the angels. In chapter 2 consider why Christ was made lower than the angels for a time.

2. Like Elijah, other faithful servants of God have become short-sighted and filled with despair. When our faith in God's power is gone, we lose our confidence and run from that which really shouldn't intimidate us. Opposition can paralyze us with fear and prevent us from proclaiming God's truth. Read Matthew 10:24-33. What did Jesus tell the disciples? If you have an antagonistic co-worker, neighbor, or relative, pray that God will give you boldness to speak the truth in love.

9
God's Invisible Army—Part 3

Outline

Introduction

Review
 I. The Existence of Angels
 II. The Origin of Angels
III. The Nature of Angels
IV. The Ministry of Angels
   A. To God
   B. To Christ
   C. To Believers
     1. Watching
     2. Revealing
     3. Guiding
     4. Providing

Lesson
     5. Protecting
       a) The fiery furnace
         (1) The refusal by the Hebrew men
         (2) The rage of the king
         (3) The rescue by the angel
       b) The lions' den
       c) The tempestuous sea
     6. Delivering
       a) The apostles
       b) Peter
       c) The heroes of faith
       d) The 144,000

Introduction

An important lesson I have learned from this study on angels is the steps God has taken to make His children physically secure. That knowledge should alleviate many of the anxieties we might unfortunately tend to have about accidents, disease, or other kinds of danger. God's angels are truly amazing beings. They guide and protect us, yet those are only two of their ministries to believers.

Restoring the Angelic Song

The context of Job 38:4-6 is God's creation of the world. At the creation, "the morning stars sang together, and all the sons of God shouted for joy" (v. 7). In our previous studies (see p. 70) we learned that that is a reference to angels. Therefore we know that angels sang in the past. In Revelation 5:11-12 John says, "I beheld, and I heard the voice of many angels round about the throne and the living creatures and the elders, and the number of them was ten thousand times ten thousand, and thousands of thousands, saying with a loud voice, Worthy is the Lamb." Were they singing? Verse 9 says, "They sang a new song." Apparently the angels in heaven join the four living creatures (other angels) and the twenty-four elders (representatives of the church) in the new song. Angels are seen singing twice in the Bible—once at the creation of the world, and again at the return of Jesus Christ. But there is no record of their singing between those two events. It's as if the angels lost their song when man fell, and the only thing that will restore their song is the return of Jesus Christ.

Review

I. THE EXISTENCE OF ANGELS (see pp. 131-32)

II. THE ORIGIN OF ANGELS (see pp. 132-36)

III. THE NATURE OF ANGELS (see pp. 136-39)

IV. THE MINISTRY OF ANGELS

    A. To God (see pp. 148-53)

    B. To Christ (see pp. 153-56)

    C. To Believers

        1. Watching (see pp. 156-57)

        2. Revealing (see p. 157)

        3. Guiding (see pp. 158-59)

        4. Providing (see pp. 159-60)

Lesson

        5. Protecting

        Angels protect God's people from physical danger. The Bible gives us several illustrations of that.

a) The fiery furnace

King Nebuchadnezzar of Babylon had an ego problem—he wanted everyone in his kingdom to worship
the golden image he had set up (Dan. 3:5).

(1) The refusal by the Hebrew men

Three Hebrew young men—Shadrach, Meshach,
and Abednego—refused to worship Nebuchadnezzar's gods or his image (vv. 12-15). At their in-
dictment they said, "O Nebuchadnezzar, we are
not careful to answer thee in this matter. If it be
so, our God, whom we serve, is able to deliver us
from the burning fiery furnace, and he will deliver us out of thine hand, O king. But if not, be it
known unto thee, O king, that we will not serve
thy gods, nor worship the golden image which
thou hast set up" (vv. 16-18).

(2) The rage of the king

Nebuchadnezzar was filled with rage: "The form
of his visage [facial expression] was changed
against Shadrach, Meshach, and Abed-nego;
therefore, he spoke, and commanded that they
should heat the furnace seven times more than it
was usually heated. And he commanded the
most mighty men that were in his army to bind
Shadrach, Meshach, and Abed-nego, and to cast
them into the burning fiery furnace. Then these
men were bound in their coats, their stockings,
and their turbans, and their other garments, and
were cast into the midst of the burning fiery furnace. Therefore, because the king's commandment was urgent and the furnace exceedingly
hot, the flame of the fire slew those men that took
up Shadrach, Meshach, and Abed-nego. And
these three men, Shadrach, Meshach, and Abed-
nego, fell down bound into the midst of the burning fiery furnace" (vv. 19-23).

(3) The rescue by the angel

The narrative continues: "Nebuchadnezzar, the king, was astounded, and rose up in haste, and spoke, and said unto his counselors, Did not we cast three men, bound, into the midst of the fire? They answered and said unto the king, True, O king. He answered and said, Lo, I see four men loose, walking in the midst of the fire, and they have no hurt; and the form of the fourth is like a son of the gods. Then Nebuchadnezzar came near to the mouth of the burning fiery furnace, and spoke, and said, Shadrach, Meshach, and Abed-nego, ye servants of the Most High God, come forth, and come here. Then Shadrach, Meshach, and Abed-nego came forth from the midst of the fire. And the princes, governors, and captains, and the king's counselors, being gathered together, saw these men, upon whose bodies the fire had no power, nor was an hair of their head singed, neither were their coats changed, nor the smell of fire had passed on them. Then Nebuchadnezzar spoke, and said, Blessed be the God of Shadrach, Meshach, and Abed-nego, who hath sent his angel and delivered his servants who trusted in him" (vv. 24-28). Some people believe the fourth person was Jesus Christ, the Angel of the Lord. Nebuchadnezzar referred to him as one "like a son of the gods." This unique angel delivered those three godly men from the midst of a furnace that burned to death those who threw them in.

b) The lions' den

Angels certainly were busy in the life of Daniel and his three companions. In Daniel 6 a different king, Darius, ruled the Medo-Persian empire. He had the same problem as Nebuchadnezzar—he wanted everyone to worship him (vv. 7-9). Having caught Daniel praying to God rather than to Darius, the princes "brought Daniel, and cast him into the den of lions.

Now the [since humbled] king spoke and said unto Daniel, Thy God, whom thou servest continually, He will deliver thee" (v. 16). Darius liked Daniel and respected Daniel's God, and hoped that He would protect Daniel from the lions.

The narrative continues: "A stone was brought, and laid upon the mouth of the den; and the king sealed it with his own signet, and with the signet of his lords, that the purpose might not be changed concerning Daniel. Then the king went to his palace, and passed the night fasting; neither were instruments of music brought before him; and his sleep went from him. Then the king arose very early in the morning, and went in haste unto the den of lions. And when he came to the den, he cried with a lamentable voice unto Daniel. And the king spoke and said to Daniel, O Daniel, servant of the living God, is thy God, whom thou servest continually, able to deliver thee from the lions? Then said Daniel unto the king, O king, live forever. My God hath sent his angel, and hath shut the lions' mouths, that they have not hurt me" (vv. 17-22). God protected Daniel by sending an angel.

c) The tempestuous sea

Acts 27 details Paul's voyage to Rome. While sailing, "there arose against it [the ship] a tempestuous wind, called Euroclydon. And when the ship was caught, and could not bear up into the wind, we let her drive. And running under the lee of a certain island which is called Clauda, we had much work to secure the boat [the dinghy], which, when they had hoisted it, they used helps, undergirding the ship" (vv. 14-17).

Verse 17 says the crew feared being driven into the quicksands or *Syrtes*, a graveyard of ships on the North African coast. So, "they struck sail [lowered the sail], and so were driven. And we being exceedingly tossed with a tempest, the next day they lightened the ship; and the third day we cast out with our own hands the tackle of the ship. And when neither sun nor stars in many days appeared, and no small tempest lay on us, all hope that we should be saved was then taken away" (vv. 17-20). Without sun and stars to use as reference, they were unable to navigate. Thus they had no idea where the tempest was taking them, and they fully expected to capsize or be smashed into something.

The narrative continues: "After being long without food, Paul stood forth in the midst of them, and said . . . I exhort you to be of good cheer; for there shall be no loss of any man's life among you, but only of the ship. For there stood by me this night an angel of God, whose I am, and whom I serve, saying, Fear not, Paul, thou must be brought before Caesar; and, lo, God hath given thee all them that sail with thee" (vv. 21-24). While that ship was being driven across the Mediterranean, there might have been a legion of angels protecting everyone on board. The ship was, in fact, destroyed by the sea, but everyone made it safely to shore. It happened just as the angel said it would.

God's angels protect His people. They take care of us when we drive on the highway, and they protect our children. When I realize that God has His angels looking out for my children, I don't worry about them because angels can do things for them that I couldn't do even if I were with them.

6. Delivering

This doesn't refer to preventing trouble, but getting people out of trouble.

a) The apostles

In its infancy the church experienced tremendous growth due to the preaching of the apostles. But the Jewish leaders were upset about the church's popularity and decided to do something about it: "The high priest rose up, and all they that were with him (which is the sect of the Sadducees) and were filled with indignation, and laid their hands on the apostles, and put them in the common prison. But an angel of the Lord by night opened the prison doors, and brought them forth, and said, Go, stand and speak in the temple to the people all the words of this life. And when they heard that, they entered into the temple early in the morning, and taught. But the high priest came, and they that were with him, and called the council together, and all the senate of the children of Israel, and sent to the prison to have them brought. But when the officers came, and found them not in the prison, they returned, and told, saying, The prison truly found we shut with all safety, and the keepers standing outside before the doors; but when we had opened, we found no man within" (Acts 5:17-23). How did they get out? The angel let them out.

It's exciting to know you can't ever get yourself into a situation from which God could not remove you if He so chose. That ought to be particularly encouraging to missionaries. With boldness they can go into dangerous places knowing that God can deliver them with His angels.

b) Peter

The persecution of the early church got worse. James was executed and Peter was thrown in prison (Acts 12:2-4). "Peter, therefore, was kept in prison; but prayer was made without ceasing by the church unto God for him. And when Herod would have brought him forth, the same night Peter was sleeping between two soldiers, bound with two chains; and the keepers before the door kept the prison. And, behold, an angel of the Lord came upon him, and a light shone in the prison; and he smote Peter on the side, and raised him up, saying, Arise quickly. And his chains fell off from his hands. And the angel said unto him, Gird thyself, and bind on thy sandals. And so he did. And he saith unto him, Cast thy garment about thee, and follow me. And he went out, and followed him, and knew not that it was true which was done by the angel, but thought he saw a vision.

170

When they were past the first and the second guard, they came unto the iron gate that leadeth unto the city, which opened to them of its own accord; and they went out, and passed on through one street; and immediately the angel departed from him. And when Peter was come to himself, he said, Now I know of a surety that the Lord hath sent his angel, and hath delivered me out of the hand of Herod" (vv. 5-11).

c) The heroes of faith

Think how active God and His angels must have been in the lives of all the people referred to in Hebrews 11. They delivered Gideon, Barak, Samson, Jephthah, David, Samuel, and the prophets, "who, through faith, subdued kingdoms, wrought righteousness, obtained promises, stopped the mouths of lions, quenched the violence of fire, escaped the edge of the sword" (vv. 33-34). Throughout history angels have served God's people by protecting and delivering them.

d) The 144,000

Angels will protect God's people during the Tribulation. After the Lord removes the true church from the world, God will take 144,000 Jews, twelve thousand from every tribe of Israel, and use them as evangelists (Rev. 7:4-10). As a result all Israel will be saved (Rom. 11:26). To make sure no one hurts God's chosen evangelists, God will have His angels place a protective seal on them. John wrote, "I saw another angel ascending from the the east, having the seal of the living God; and he cried with a loud voice . . . saying, Hurt not the earth, neither the sea, nor the trees, till we have sealed the servants of our God in their foreheads" (Rev. 7:2-3). The angel sealed the 144,000 so they wouldn't be harmed during the Tribulation. Perhaps the seal is a means of identification so that the angels know whom they are to protect from the slaughter during the Tribulation.

7. Facilitating God's answers to prayer

Angels do not answer prayer, but they can be involved in bringing about the answer God desires.

a) An example

The angel who took Peter out of prison did so in response to the fervent prayers of the church (Acts 12:5); God sent the angel to deliver Peter in answer to those prayers. Daniel 9:20-27 and 10:10-14 are other examples of God sending answers to prayer with an angel.

b) A warning

Let me add that we do not pray to angels because they don't exercise their own will independently of God. They are only servants—they obey God. Prayer offered to God is the only prayer ever heard. But God may discharge or activate His angels to bring about a response to that prayer.

8. Attending deaths

Billy Graham wrote, "Hundreds of accounts record the heavenly escort of angels at death. When my maternal grandmother died, for instance, the room seemed to fill with a heavenly light. She sat up in bed and almost laughingly said, 'I see Jesus . . . and I see the angels' " (*Angels: God's Secret Agents* [Garden City, N.Y.: Doubleday, 1975], p. 152).

Does Scripture support such claims? Luke 16:19-22 says, "There was a certain rich man, who was clothed in purple and fine linen, and fared sumptuously every day. And there was a certain beggar, named Lazarus, who was laid at his gate, full of sores, and desiring to be fed with the crumbs which fell from the rich man's table; moreover, the dogs came and licked his sores. And it came to pass that the beggar died, and was carried by the angels into Abraham's bosom." That man may not have been significant to anyone in the world, but when he died, God dispatched His angels to take him to heaven.

9. Gathering the elect

Angels will minister to the Tribulation saints—those who will be redeemed during that period. When Jesus returns, "He shall send his angels with a great sound of a trumpet, and they shall gather together his elect" (Matt. 24:31). The angels will gather all the saints together.

10. Serving

During the millennial kingdom, angels will serve us as we rule. First Corinthians 6:2-3 says, "Do ye not know that the saints shall judge the world? . . . Know ye not that we shall judge [rule over] angels?" In the coming kingdom we will rule with Christ as co-regents and joint heirs (Matt. 19:28; Rom. 8:17). The angels will be subject to us.

What should be our attitude toward angels? We ought to respect them as holy servants of God. We ought to appreciate them, knowing how they help us. And we ought to follow their example of continual worship and service to God.

Should We Worship Angels?

While we can be appreciative of angels and follow their example, we should not worship them because that is sin. Angels don't want our worship, and Scripture forbids the worship of angels.

1. Colossians 2:18—"Let no man beguile you of your reward in a voluntary humility and worshiping of angels." Don't let anyone trick you into worshiping angels.

2. Revelation 19:10—The apostle John fell down at the feet of an angel to worship him, but the angel said to him, "See thou do it not! I am thy your fellow servant. . . . Worship God."

173

3. Revelation 22:8-9—John obviously was a little slow in learning his lesson: "I fell down to worship before the feet of the angel who showed me these things. Then saith he unto me, See thou do it not; for I am thy fellow servant. . . . Worship God."

What do angels ask from us? Only that we worship God. Angels are but an extension of God's love, care, power, grace, and provision. All the glory belongs to God, not to angels, and they wouldn't have it any other way.

D. To Unbelievers

How do angels operate in the lives of unbelievers? Only one way—they are God's executioners. They were involved in the destruction of Sodom and Gomorrah (Gen. 19). They brought judgment on Egypt as executioners of the Egyptian first-born (Ex. 12:23, 29). One angel killed 185,000 Assyrian soldiers in answer to the prayer of Hezekiah (2 Kings 19:14-20, 35).

1. In the past

In Acts 12 we are introduced to Herod Agrippa I, grandson of Herod the Great. This Herod was so proud that he established a national holiday to honor himself. Displeased with the existing political situation, Herod took what was supposed to be Roman emperor's commemoration day and turned it into his own day. Acts 12:21-23 says, "Upon a set day Herod, arrayed in royal apparel, sat upon his throne, and made an oration unto them. And the people gave a shout, saying, It is the voice of a god, and not a man. And immediately an angel of the Lord smote him, because he gave not God the glory; and he was eaten of worms, and died."

2. In the future

Throughout Revelation 6-19 angels appear as emissaries of judgment.

a) Revelation 8:7–9:1—"The first angel sounded, and there followed hail and fire mixed with blood, and they were cast upon the earth; and the third part of

174

trees were burnt up, and all green grass was burnt up. And the second angel sounded, and, as it were, a great mountain burning with fire was cast into the sea; and the third part of the sea became blood; and the third part of the creatures which were in the sea, and had life, died; and the third part of the ships were destroyed. And the third angel sounded, and there fell a great star from heaven, burning as though it were a lamp, and it fell upon the third part of the rivers, and upon the fountains of waters. And the name of the star is called Wormwood; and the third part of the waters became wormwood; and many men died of the waters, because they were made bitter. And the fourth angel sounded, and the third part of the sun was smitten, and the third part of the moon, and the third part of the stars, so that the third part of them was darkened, and the day shone not for a third part of it, and the night likewise. And I beheld, and heard an angel flying through the midst of heaven, saying with a loud voice, Woe, woe, woe, to the inhabiters of the earth by reason of the other voices of the trumpet of the three angels, which are yet to sound! And the fifth angel sounded, and I saw a star fall from heaven unto the earth; and to him was given the key of the bottomless pit." The text goes on to explain what happens as a result of the last three trumpets and the terrible judgments that accompany them.

b) Revelation 16:2-4, 8, 10-11—The following is just a sampling of what happens when the bowls of wrath are poured out on the earth: "The first went, and poured out his bowl upon the earth, and there fell a foul and painful sore upon the men. . . . And the second angel poured out his bowl upon the sea, and it became like the blood of a dead man; and every living soul died in the sea. And the third angel poured out his bowl upon the rivers and fountains of waters, and they became blood. . . . And the fourth angel poured out his bowl upon the sun, and power was given unto him to scorch men with fire. . . . And the fifth angel poured out his bowl upon the throne of the beast, and his kingdom was full of darkness; and they gnawed their tongues for pain, and blasphemed the God of heaven because of their pains and their sores, and repented not of their deeds." The two final bowls bring further judgment.

c) 2 Thessalonians 1:7-9—"To you who are troubled, rest with us, when the Lord Jesus shall be revealed from heaven with his mighty angels, in flaming fire taking vengeance on them that know not God, and that obey not the gospel of our Lord Jesus Christ; who shall be punished with everlasting destruction from the presence of the Lord, and from the glory of his power."

d) Matthew 13:41-42—"The Son of man shall send forth his angels, and they shall gather out of his kingdom all things that offend, and them who do iniquity, and shall cast them into a furnace of fire; there shall be wailing and gnashing of teeth."

e) Matthew 25:41—"Then shall he say also unto them on the left hand, Depart from me, ye cursed, into everlasting fire, prepared for the devil and his angels." The ungodly will spend eternity with the fallen angels. And their judgment will be carried out by "the Son of man . . . and all the holy angels" (v. 31).

Conclusion

It's tragic to think about the options: you receive either the ministry of angels given to believers, or that given to unbelievers. Each of us chooses which ministry we will receive. If you receive Jesus Christ as your Lord and Savior, the angels will perform a work of watching, revealing, guiding, protecting, providing, delivering, bringing answers to prayer, and carrying you into heaven. But if you reject Jesus Christ, the angels will cast you into hell.

The angels much prefer it if you turn to Christ. Luke 15:8-10 says, "What woman, having ten pieces of silver, if she lose one piece, doth not light a lamp, and sweep the house, and seek diligently till she find it? And when she hath found it, she calleth her friends and her neighbors together, saying, Rejoice with me; for I have found the piece which I had lost. Likewise, I say unto you, there is joy in the presence of the angels of God over one sinner that repenteth." The angels would much rather care for you as a believer than judge you as an unbeliever.

Focusing on the Facts

1. What made Shadrach, Meshach, and Abednego willing to suffer the consequences of disobeying the law (Dan. 3:16-18; see p. 166)?
2. After the angel released the apostles, what command did he give that the apostles followed (Acts 5:19-21; see pp. 169-70)?
3. What did Peter first think was happening when the angel miraculously delivered him (Acts 12:9; see pp. 170-71)?
4. During the Tribulation, how will the 144,000 Jewish evangelists be protected (see p. 171)?
5. How will angels minister to believers right after the Tribulation (Matt. 24:31; see p. 173)?
6. What position will glorified believers have that will cause the angels to be subject to them in the millennial kingdom (Rom. 8:17; 1 Cor. 6:2-3; see p. 173)?
7. Why shouldn't we worship angels (see pp. 173-74)?
8. Why was Herod Agrippa I struck down by an angel (Acts 12:23; see p. 174)?
9. How will angels carry out God's judgment (see pp. 174-76)?
10. What causes joy among the angels (Luke 15:10; see pp. 176-77)?

Pondering the Principles

1. Review the section about the tempestuous sea (see pp. 168-69). After many days of being at the storm's mercy, "all hope . . . was then taken away" (Acts 27:20). Sometimes God has to bring people to the depths of despair before they will look to Him. There may be people around you who have lost all hope in their work, marriage, or children. Pray for sensitivity to their needs and that God might use you to offer them words of hope from Scripture.

2. Many times people refuse to listen to the wise counsel of a godly man or woman. Some disregarded Paul's angelic promise and

worried about their own safety (Acts 27:30), but Paul made it clear that his advice must be followed for God's promise to be fulfilled (vv. 31-32). Verse 44 says that all 276 people on board "were brought safely to land" (NASB). When we are faithful to obey, God is faithful in fulfilling His promises to us. Is there any area of your life where you have failed to obey God's Word? Strive to be more like the centurion, who, although he didn't believe Paul at first (v. 11), finally realized that he should trust him (vv. 31-32). Have respect for the godly people in your life and be sure to carefully consider what they say.

3. Many in the church prayed fervently for God to release Peter when he was in prison (Acts 12:5). But when he was miraculously released by the angel, many of those who prayed for it didn't believe it had happened (vv. 15-16). Are you praying for something you don't expect God to do? Are you merely going through the motions of prayer? Be faithful in your prayers and don't be surprised when God answers them. Read what Jesus had to say about the miraculous power of prayer in Mark 11:23-24; Luke 11:5-10, 18:1-8; and John 15:7.

Scripture Index

184

Topical Index

trusting, 64-65
unchangeableness of. *See* immutability of
wisdom of. *See* omniscience of
wrath of, 10, 24, 36-37, 43, 61-62. *See also* Judgment
Graham, Billy
his belief in angels, 130
his grandmother's death, 172
John Paton's angelic deliverance, 127

Holiness
God's. *See* God
pursuing, 63, 65
motivation for, 35-37, 44-45
Hope, basis of, 41
Humility, basis of, 42
Hypocrisy, futility of, 57

Idolatry
definition of, 29-30
satanically inspired, 112-13
Illness
protection from, 164
satanically inspired, 114
Immutability of God. *See* God
Indifference, result of, 109
Integrity, motivation for, 36

Jesus Christ
angel of the Lord. *See* Angel of the Lord
equality with God, 22, 26
Judgment
angelic involvement in, 174-76
basis of, 57-58
See also God, wrath of

Life, highest pursuit of, 49-50
Lucifer. *See* Satan

Lust, satanically inspired, 113-14

MacArthur, John, football strategies played by, 69
Man, highest pursuit of, 49-50
Mental illness. *See* Illness
Mercy, God's. *See* God
Miracles, satanically inspired, 76, 98
Moderation. *See* Balance
Murder, satanically inspired, 92-93

Occultic practices, 76, 94, 130
Omnipotence of God. *See* God
Omnipresence of God. *See* God
Omniscience of God. *See* God
Ontological argument. *See* God, existence of
Ott, Ludwig, on venerating angels, 129
Ouija boards. *See* Occultic practices

Paton, John, his preservation by angels, 127
Paul, angelic protection of, 168-69, 177-78
Pentecost, J. Dwight, on preachers controlled by Satan, 110
Persecution
protection from. *See* Protection
satanically inspired, 116
Peter, angelic protection of, 170-71
Power, lusting after, 86
Prayer
angels and, 172
expectant, 178

Theophany, 147. *See also* Angel of the Lord
Tozer, A. W.
  on knowing God, 29
  on the omnipotence of God, 38
Trinity, the
  illustrations of, 21
  in the New Testament, 20-21
  in the Old Testament, 20, 148. *See also* Angel of the Lord
  mystery of, 21
Trusting God. *See* God
Twain, Mark, despair of, 15

UFOs, 127, 130

Victory, basis of, 41
Voltaire, despair of, 15

Von Gerdteil, Dr., on the existence of Satan, 73

Warfare, spiritual
  among Christians, 116-23
  among non-Christians, 107-16, 124
  call to, 84
  reality of, 84
  strategy for, 69
  See also Temptation, Satan
Wells, H. G., despair of, 15
Witchcraft. *See* Occultic practices
Worry. *See* Anxiety
Worship
  of angels. *See* Angels
  basis of, 40

235 MAC   3552

God, Satan, and Angels
MacArthur, John Jr

©1989
Oxford University